HANOI

Travel Guide 2025

Exploring the Top Attractions, Hidden Gems, Authentic Cuisine, and Budget Tips for the Ultimate Vietnamese Experience

Arden M. Grey

Copyright © 2025 Arden M. Grey All rights reserved.

No part of this book may be reproduced, stored in a retrieval system, or transmitted in any form or by any means, electronic, mechanical, photocopying, recording, or otherwise, without the publisher's prior written permission, except for brief quotations used in reviews.

Disclaimer:

The information contained in this book is for general informational purposes only. The author and publisher make no representations or warranties concerning the content's accuracy, applicability, or completeness. The author and publisher disclaim any liability arising directly or indirectly from the use of this book.

TABLE OF CONTENT

INTRODUCTION 9

Hanoi at a Glance: Why Visit Vietnam's Capital 11

2. Top 5 Reasons to Explore Hanoi 12

3. When to Visit: Weather, Festivals, and Seasons 14

4. Planning Essentials: Visas, Currency, and Local Etiquette 16

CHAPTER 1 24

Getting Started – Arrival in Hanoi 24

1 Airports, Trains, and Bus Terminals: Navigating Entry Points 24

2. Transportation Tips: Taxis, Motorbikes, and Public Transit 31

3. First Impressions: Settling into the City 38

4. Staying Safe: Travel Insurance, Emergency Numbers, and Local Laws 39

CHAPTER 2 42

Iconic Hanoi – Must-See Attractions 42

Hoan Kiem Lake: Legends and Landmarks 42

2. The Old Quarter: A Walk Through History 46

3. Ho Chi Minh Mausoleum and Museum 49

4. Temple of Literature: Exploring Vietnam's Heritage 52

CHAPTER 3 56

Accommodation Options for Every Traveler 56

1. Luxury Stays: Hanoi's Top-Rated Hotels and Resorts
.... 56

2. Budget-Friendly Choices: Hostels and Guesthouses 64

3. Boutique Hotels and Homestays: A Cultural Experience 67

4. Choosing the Right Neighborhood: Old Quarter, Tay Ho, and Beyond 74

CHAPTER 4 80

A Taste of Hanoi – Food and Drink 80

1. Hanoi's Iconic Dishes: Pho, Bun Cha, and Beyond .. 80

2. Best Street Food Spots: Hidden Gems and Famous Eateries 83

3. Cafés and Unique Beverages: Egg Coffee and Tea Houses 88

4. Food Tours and Cooking Classes: Learn and Indulge
.... 90

CHAPTER 5 96

Shopping and Souvenirs 96

Hanoi's Best Markets: Dong Xuan and Night Markets 96

2. Authentic Souvenirs: Silk, Art, and Handicrafts 100

3. Exploring Boutiques and Local Designers 104

4. Tips for Bargaining Like a Local 108

CHAPTER 6 111

Beyond the City – Hanoi's Day Trips 111

Ha Long Bay: Majestic Waters and Limestone Cliffs 111

2. Ninh Binh: Pagodas, Rice Fields, and Boat Rides .. 114

3. Perfume Pagoda: A Scenic Pilgrimage 118

4. Bat Trang Ceramic Village: Traditional Craftsmanship 121

CHAPTER 7 125

Nature and Relaxation in Hanoi 125

1. Hoan Kiem Lake and West Lake: Scenic Escapes .. 125

2. Hanoi's Green Spaces: Parks, Gardens, and Hidden Retreats 128

3. Rooftop Bars and Cafés: Unwind with a View 131

4. Wellness and Spa Experiences in the City 135

CHAPTER 8 138

Adventure and Activities in Hanoi 138

1. Motorbike Tours: Thrills on Two Wheels 138

2. Walking Trails and Urban Exploration 141

3. Hanoi's Hidden Gems: From Secret Alleys to Rooftop Views 145

4. Seasonal Festivals: Celebrating Hanoi's Vibrant Culture 148

CHAPTER 9 151

The Perfect 5-Day Itinerary 151

1. Day 1: Arrival, Exploring the Old Quarter, and a Street Food Tour 151

2. Day 2: Historical Sites and Lakeside Relaxation 154

3. Day 3: A Day Trip to Ha Long Bay or Ninh Binh .. 157

4. Day 4: Shopping, Cafés, and Hidden Spots 161

5. Day 5: Farewell Hanoi – A Relaxing Morning Before Departure 164

CHAPTER 10 167

Insider Tips and Resources 167

1. Seasonal Packing Guide for Hanoi 167

2. Apps and Tools for a Seamless Trip 170

3. How to Respect Local Customs and Culture 173

4. Contact Directory: Embassies, Hospitals, and Tourist Assistance 175

CONCLUSION 179

SCAN THIS QR CODE TO GET YOUR HANOI MAP

After scanner the QR Code you will be linked directly to your Google Maps app, where you can now input your current location and click direction to get the exact direction from your current location to your hotel or your destination this is why you sue better scanner the QR Code for more information

INTRODUCTION

Hanoi is a city that breathes history, culture, and a unique charm that captures the essence of Vietnam. In 2025, this bustling metropolis is more than just a destination—it's an experience waiting to unfold. From the narrow lanes of the Old Quarter to the tranquil beauty of Hoan Kiem Lake, Hanoi offers a blend of old-world charm and modern sophistication that will leave a lasting impression.

The city's streets are filled with energy, yet there's an undeniable sense of calm that permeates the air, especially when you stop to savor a bowl of pho at a local street vendor or wander through the quiet courtyards of its ancient temples. Hanoi's rich heritage is not only seen in its architecture but is also reflected in the warm hospitality of its people, who have kept their traditions alive while embracing the future with open arms.

Whether you're seeking to explore historical landmarks, enjoy local delicacies, or simply soak in the vibrant atmosphere, Hanoi has something for everyone. The city is home to remarkable landmarks like the Ho Chi Minh Mausoleum, the Temple of Literature, and the serene West Lake, each offering a glimpse into the country's past and present. Add to this the ever-growing café culture and lively markets, and you'll find yourself immersed in a city that knows how to balance tradition with modernity.

This guide to Hanoi 2025 is your personal gateway to the heart of Vietnam's capital. With insider tips, essential travel information, and recommendations for every type of traveler, it's designed to help you experience Hanoi in all its beauty, culture, and excitement. Whether you're a history buff, a foodie, or simply someone looking to enjoy the buzz of a city full of life, Hanoi is sure to leave you with memories that will last a lifetime.

Get ready to explore, to taste, to see—and to experience the magic of Hanoi like never before.

Let Started

Hanoi at a Glance: Why Visit Vietnam's Capital

Hanoi is a city that pulls you in with its quiet charm and vibrant energy. As Vietnam's capital, it offers a glimpse into the country's past, present, and future. The Old Quarter is a maze of narrow streets where the old-world charm is palpable. Here, you'll find colonial-era buildings, bustling markets, and street vendors serving pho that seems to tell its own story.

Beyond its historic sites, Hanoi is also a city that's alive with creativity and culture. From the serene beauty of Hoan Kiem Lake to the tranquility of West Lake, Hanoi offers spaces to relax and unwind, while its many museums and galleries showcase the country's rich heritage and contemporary art scene. Whether you're wandering through the Temple of Literature or visiting the Ho Chi Minh Mausoleum, every corner of the city feels like it has something to say.

Hanoi is also a food lover's dream. The street food culture here is unlike anywhere else, with each dish a flavorful reflection of the city's history. From traditional Vietnamese meals like banh mi to local sweets and snacks, eating your way through Hanoi is an experience in itself.

What sets Hanoi apart is how it balances the old with the new. In this city, history and modernity don't clash—they complement each other, creating a place that's both timeless and forward-thinking. Whether you're here for the culture, the food, or just the energy of the city, Hanoi's magnetic pull will make it hard to leave.

2. Top 5 Reasons to Explore Hanoi

Hanoi, Vietnam's capital, is a city that blends history, culture, and modern energy in ways that captivate anyone who steps into it. Here are five reasons why exploring Hanoi should be at the top of your list.

1. Rich History and Culture
Hanoi is steeped in history. From the iconic Ho Chi Minh Mausoleum to the ancient Temple of Literature, the city is a treasure trove of cultural landmarks. Each site tells a story that spans centuries, offering visitors a deeper understanding of Vietnam's heritage.

2. Unmatched Street Food Scene
Vietnamese food is known worldwide, but in Hanoi, it reaches another level. The streets are lined with food vendors

offering fresh, authentic dishes like pho, banh mi, and egg coffee. The flavors here are unlike anything you've tasted before, and every meal feels like a new discovery.

3. Charming Old Quarter

The Old Quarter of Hanoi is a maze of narrow streets that hum with life. The French colonial architecture, the hustle of local markets, and the aromas of street food create an unforgettable sensory experience. It's a place where old traditions and modern influences meet, making it one of Hanoi's most interesting areas to explore.

4. Natural Beauty

Despite its urban vibe, Hanoi is also home to peaceful spaces like Hoan Kiem Lake and West Lake, offering moments of serenity amid the city's hustle. The calm waters and surrounding parks provide a relaxing escape and an opportunity to connect with nature.

5. Vibrant Local Life

The true heart of Hanoi lies in its people. The locals are warm, friendly, and proud of their city. Whether you're chatting with a street vendor or exploring a local market, you'll get a taste of Hanoi's everyday life, making your visit even more memorable.

In short, Hanoi offers a blend of history, food, culture, and natural beauty that makes it a city worth exploring.

3. When to Visit: Weather, Festivals, and Seasons

Hanoi's weather offers a mix of experiences, each season bringing its own charm. Understanding the climate can help you plan the perfect time to explore this vibrant city.

Spring (March to April)
Spring in Hanoi is a beautiful time to visit. Temperatures are mild, usually ranging from 15°C to 25°C (59°F to 77°F), making it comfortable for sightseeing. The air is fresh, and the city's parks and lakes are full of blooming flowers, especially the iconic peach blossoms. This is also the time when the Lunar New Year (Tết) festivities often take place, filling the city with colorful celebrations and a lively atmosphere.

Summer (May to August)

Hanoi's summer months can be hot and humid, with temperatures reaching up to 35°C (95°F). The humidity can make the heat feel even more intense, but it's also when the city's outdoor cafes and lakesides come alive. If you're planning to visit during this time, early mornings and evenings are the best times to explore. June to August also brings the Hanoi International Film Festival, a highlight for cinephiles looking to catch some of the world's best films.

Autumn (September to November)

Autumn is often considered the best time to visit Hanoi. The weather is cooler, with temperatures around 20°C to 25°C (68°F to 77°F). The sky is clear, and the city's streets are less crowded than in the summer. Hanoi's autumn is also marked by the Mid-Autumn Festival, a beloved event full of lantern displays, mooncakes, and family gatherings, adding a touch of magic to the atmosphere.

Winter (December to February)

Winter in Hanoi is cool, with temperatures dropping to around 10°C (50°F) in the mornings and evenings. This is the quietest season in terms of tourism, so you'll have a more peaceful experience exploring the city's museums, temples, and markets. The chilly air also brings an opportunity to enjoy warm Vietnamese dishes like hot pho and grilled skewers.

Each season in Hanoi has its own personality, making it a city worth visiting year-round.

4. Planning Essentials: Visas, Currency, and Local Etiquette

Planning a trip to Hanoi involves understanding Vietnam's visa and entry protocols. This guide provides detailed information to ensure a smooth journey.

I. Types of Visas

Visa Requirements for Hanoi
Vietnam offers various visa options tailored to different travel purposes:
- Tourist Visa (DL): For leisure travelers.
- Business Visa (DN): For business-related activities.
- E-Visa: An electronic visa available to citizens of 80 countries, valid for up to 90 days with single or multiple entries.

Who Needs a Visa to Visit Hanoi?

Visa requirements depend on nationality:
- Visa-Exempt Countries: Citizens from 25 countries can enter Vietnam without a visa for stays ranging from 14 to 45 days. For example, citizens of the United Kingdom, Germany, France, Spain, Italy, Russia, Belarus, Norway, Sweden, Denmark, and Finland are exempted for a 45-day stay.
- E-Visa Eligible Countries: Nationals from 80 countries can apply for an e-visa.
- Others: Citizens not covered by the above categories must obtain a visa prior to arrival.

II. Applying for a Visa to Hanoi

Where to Apply
- E-Visa: Apply online through Vietnam's official e-visa portal:
- Embassy/Consulate: For other visa types, apply at the nearest Vietnamese embassy or consulate. For instance, in the United States:

- Embassy of Vietnam in Washington, D.C.: 1233 20th Street NW, Suite 400, Washington, D.C. 20036
- Consulate General of Vietnam in San Francisco: 1700 California Street, Suite 580, San Francisco, CA 94109

When to Apply

- E-Visa: Apply at least 3-5 business days before departure.
- Embassy/Consulate Visa: Apply 1-2 months in advance to accommodate processing times.

What Documents Do You Need?

- Completed Visa Application Form
- Valid Passport: Must have at least six months' validity and two blank pages.
- Passport-Sized Photo: Recent and compliant with specifications.
- Travel Itinerary: Including flight bookings and accommodation details.
- Proof of Funds: To demonstrate financial capability.
- Visa Fee Payment Receipt

Visa Processing Time

- E-Visa: Typically processed within 3 working days.

- Embassy/Consulate Visa: Processing times vary; generally between 5-7 working days.

Visa Fees

- E-Visa: $25 USD for single-entry; $50 USD for multiple-entry.
- Embassy/Consulate Visa: Fees vary based on visa type and duration; consult the specific embassy or consulate for accurate information.

III. Entering Hanoi

What Documents Do You Need to Enter Hanoi?

- Valid Passport
- Approved Visa or E-Visa Printout
- Return or Onward Travel Ticket
- Proof of Accommodation
- Sufficient Funds for the Duration of Stay

Passport Control

Upon arrival, present your passport and visa to immigration officers. Ensure all documents are in order to facilitate a smooth entry.

Visa Checks

Immigration officials will verify your visa details. For e-visa holders, a printout of the e-visa approval is required.

Other Documents You May Need

- Vaccination Certificates: Depending on health regulations.
- Travel Insurance: Recommended for unforeseen circumstances.

IV. Visa Extensions

How to Extend Your Visa in Hanoi

To extend your stay:
- Visit the Vietnam Immigration Department: Located at 44-46 Tran Phu Street, Ba Dinh District, Hanoi.
- Submit Required Documents: Including your passport, current visa, and a completed NA5 application form.
- Pay the Extension Fee: Fees vary based on the extension period.

When to Apply

Apply at least 5-7 days before your current visa expires to allow sufficient processing time.

What Documents Do You Need?
- Valid Passport
- Current Visa
- Completed NA5 Application Form
- Passport-Sized Photos
- Proof of Residence in Vietnam
- Proof of Financial Means

Visa Extension Fees
Fees depend on the extension duration and visa type. Consult the Vietnam Immigration Department for precise information.

V. Leaving Hanoi
What Documents Do You Need to Leave Hanoi?
- Valid Passport
- Valid Visa or Visa Extension
- Departure Card: Usually provided upon arrival; ensure it's retained for departure.

Passport Control

Present your passport and departure card to immigration officers upon exiting.

Visa Checks

Officials will verify that your visa or extension is valid and that you have not overstayed.

Other Documents You May Need

- Boarding Pass
- Customs Declarations: If applicable.

Currency and Money Matters

The official currency is the Vietnamese dong (VND). Although credit cards are widely accepted in larger establishments, cash is still king in many smaller shops, markets, and street food vendors. ATMs are easily found across Hanoi, and it's advisable to carry small denominations for everyday purchases. Familiarize yourself with exchange rates before arrival to avoid confusion.

Local Etiquette

Hanoi is a city where traditions hold a special place, and showing respect for local customs is highly appreciated.

Dress modestly when visiting temples or pagodas—covered shoulders and knees are a must. When greeting locals, a friendly nod or slight bow works well. Avoid public displays of affection, as they are considered inappropriate in Vietnamese culture. When dining, always leave some food on your plate as a sign you are satisfied, and never stick chopsticks upright in your bowl, as it's linked to funeral rites.

By understanding these essentials, you'll be ready to navigate Hanoi confidently and enjoy the warmth and hospitality of its people.

CHAPTER 1

Getting Started – Arrival in Hanoi

Your journey to Hanoi begins the moment you step off the plane, train, or bus into its energetic streets. This chapter provides all you need to know about navigating Hanoi's entry points, finding reliable transportation, and settling in smoothly. Stay informed with tips on safety, local laws, and essential first impressions.

1 Airports, Trains, and Bus Terminals: Navigating Entry Points

Arriving in Hanoi, Vietnam's bustling capital, is a straightforward process, whether you're flying in, catching a train, or arriving by bus. The city is well-served by a variety of transportation options that connect it to both local and international destinations. Here's your complete guide to entering Hanoi through its airports, trains, and bus terminals.

Noi Bai International Airport (HAN)

The Noi Bai International Airport (IATA: HAN) is the primary international gateway to Hanoi. Located about 30 kilometers (18 miles) north of the city center, this airport handles both international and domestic flights, making it the go-to entry point for travelers. The airport is modern and efficient, with good facilities for both domestic and international passengers.

Direct Flights and Travel Times

Numerous international flights connect Hanoi with major cities worldwide, including Bangkok, Hong Kong, Singapore, and Seoul. From Europe, popular hubs like Paris and London offer direct flights to Hanoi, typically with a travel time of around 11–12 hours from the UK or France. Asian cities such as Tokyo or Kuala Lumpur have relatively short flights to Hanoi, taking about 6–7 hours. If you're flying in from the US, connecting flights are common, with layovers in cities like Hong Kong or Bangkok, before making the final leg of the journey to Hanoi.

Check flight comparison websites like https://www.google.com/flights), https://www.skyscanner.com), and https://www.kayak.com) for the best prices and options. Round-trip prices from major cities can range from $400 to $1,200 USD, depending on the season and how early you book.

Immigration and Luggage Claims

Once you've landed, proceed to immigration where you'll show your passport and any required documentation (visa, onward ticket, etc.). Citizens of many countries can obtain a Visa on Arrival, while others may need to arrange a visa in advance through the http://www.xuatnhapcanh.gov.vn/en).

After clearing immigration, head to the baggage claim area, where you can collect your luggage. The baggage area is well-marked with clear English signs to help guide you through the process.

Car Hire at Noi Bai Airport

For those wishing to rent a car, several international car rental agencies operate directly at Noi Bai International Airport, including Avis, Budget, and Europcar. The car rental desks are located in the arrival hall of the airport, offering a convenient way to get started with your journey in Hanoi. However, keep in mind that while the convenience of renting a car may appeal, driving conditions in Hanoi can be challenging. The traffic is chaotic, and the roads are often crowded with motorbikes, bicycles, and cars all competing for space. If you are not familiar with the local driving style, it might be more comfortable and safer to opt for other forms of transport.

Avis Car Rental

Address: Noi Bai International Airport, Arrival Hall

Phone: +84 24 3826 3088

Website: https://www.avis.com.vn)

Budget Car Rental

Address: Noi Bai International Airport, Arrival Hall

Phone: +84 24 3838 0065

Website: https://www.budget.vn)

Connecting Flights via Major Hubs

If you're flying to Hanoi from farther away, connecting flights are available through several major Asian and European hubs. Some of the most frequent transit points for international travelers include Hong Kong International, Singapore Changi, Bangkok Suvarnabhumi, and Kuala Lumpur International. Airlines such as Vietnam Airlines, Cathay Pacific, Singapore Airlines, and Thai Airways often route their flights through these major hubs, offering convenient connections.

For European travelers, Paris Charles de Gaulle and London Heathrow are also popular stopovers for flights heading to Hanoi. Booking your flight through these hubs typically involves a quick transfer and a short layover, making it an easy and efficient journey.

Other Transportation Entry Points: Trains and Bus Terminals

Though Noi Bai International Airport is the primary entry point for international visitors, Hanoi is also accessible by train and bus from various locations within Vietnam.

Trains:

The Hanoi Railway Station (Ga Ha Noi) is the main hub for trains arriving from cities across Vietnam, including Hue, Danang, and Ho Chi Minh City. Trains are a comfortable way to travel within Vietnam, offering overnight sleeper options as well as daytime services. For long-distance travel, it's advisable to book your tickets in advance through the official [Vietnam Railways website](http://www.dsvn.vn).

Bus Terminals:

Hanoi has several bus terminals, with the Giáp Bát and Mỹ Đình stations being the largest for buses traveling from nearby cities. The buses are a more budget-friendly option, but the journey can be longer than by train or plane. Major bus companies like The Sinh Tourist and Futa Bus offer services to and from Hanoi from cities like Ho Chi Minh City, Ninh Binh, and Hai Phong.

Airport Facilities and Currency Exchange

Noi Bai International Airport is well-equipped for international travelers. It features free Wi-Fi, lounges for a more relaxed waiting experience, and a variety of duty-free shops selling both local and international goods. There are also several currency exchange counters and ATMs at the airport, where you can withdraw Vietnamese Dong (VND) directly or exchange your foreign currency. Currency exchange rates are generally competitive, but you may find better rates in the city.

ATMs are available in the Arrival Hall, and they accept most international debit and credit cards. If you need cash immediately, it's recommended to use an ATM rather than exchange currency at the airport, as the rates are usually better.

Transportation from Noi Bai Airport to the City Center

Once you've arrived and cleared all formalities, you'll need to get from the airport to your accommodation in Hanoi's city center. Thankfully, there are several convenient options available:

1. Taxis:

Taxis are available outside the Arrival Hall, with fares to downtown Hanoi ranging from 300,000 to 400,000 VND (approximately $13–$18 USD). Always use official airport taxis, which you can recognize by their clearly marked signs. The journey typically takes 30–40 minutes, depending on traffic.

2. Ride-Hailing Services:

Services like Grab operate in Hanoi and are a popular choice for many visitors. You can book a ride through the Grab app and expect a fare of around 200,000 VND (approximately $8 USD) to the city center.

3. Airport Shuttle Buses:

For budget-conscious travelers, the Airport Shuttle Bus is a convenient and affordable option. The fare is approximately 40,000 VND (around $2 USD) per person. The journey can take around 45 minutes to an hour, depending on traffic, and buses depart every 30 minutes from the airport.

4. Private Car Services:

Many hotels and local companies offer private transfers that can be booked in advance. This option is more expensive, typically costing around 500,000 to 600,000 VND (roughly $20–$25 USD), but it offers the convenience of a direct ride to your accommodation.

In conclusion, Hanoi's transportation network is well-equipped to handle international and domestic travelers. Whether you're flying in, arriving by train, or taking a bus, getting to the city center is relatively straightforward. Just be sure to plan your arrival in advance, and use reliable services to ensure a smooth and enjoyable start to your adventure in Vietnam's capital.

2. Transportation Tips: Taxis, Motorbikes, and Public Transit

Getting around Hanoi is part of the adventure. Whether you're hailing a taxi, jumping on a motorbike, or hopping onto public transport, there are plenty of options to help you explore the city with ease. For many visitors, taxis are one of the most comfortable and straightforward ways to travel, but knowing how to navigate the system can make a big difference. Here's everything you need to know about taxis in Hanoi.

Taxi Companies in Hanoi

Hanoi has a variety of reliable taxi companies, each offering safe and comfortable rides. Some of the most common and trustworthy ones include:

- Mai Linh Taxi: One of the most reputable companies in Hanoi, Mai Linh taxis are easily recognized by their green and white color scheme. They are known for their consistent service and metered fares.
- Vinasun Taxi: Another well-known company in Vietnam, Vinasun offers modern cars and excellent service, marked by their red and white colors.
- Airport Taxi (Noi Bai): These taxis are specifically for airport transfers, and the drivers are well-versed in handling tourist routes to and from Noi Bai International Airport.

Other smaller companies also operate in the city, but it's best to stick with the major ones for a more secure experience.

Types of Tickets and Prices

Taxis in Hanoi operate using meters, which is the standard method of fare calculation. Prices are generally quite reasonable compared to taxis in other major cities, but it's always good to have an idea of what to expect:

- Flag fall (starting fee): Around 12,000 VND (approx. $0.50 USD).
- Per kilometer charge: Approximately 15,000 to 20,000 VND (about $0.60 to $0.80 USD).
- Night-time or special surcharges: Some companies may charge a slight additional fee for rides after midnight or for longer distances.

A typical fare from Hanoi Old Quarter to West Lake should cost around 100,000 VND (roughly $4 USD), while a trip to Noi Bai International Airport could range from 300,000 to 400,000 VND (around $12 to $16 USD), depending on traffic conditions.

Operating Hours

Taxis in Hanoi run 24 hours a day, although during the late-night hours, you may have to wait a little longer to hail one. Most taxi companies offer 24-hour service, so you can always get a ride no matter what time you need to head out. However, during rush hours (typically 7:30–9:00 AM and 4:30–6:30 PM), taxis can be in high demand, so expect longer wait times or difficulty hailing one on the street.

Where to Find Taxis
- Taxi Stands: Taxis can be found at major hotels, shopping malls, and tourist attractions throughout the city. For example, Hanoi Opera House or West Lake are popular locations with plenty of taxis available. You can also find taxi ranks at train stations and bus terminals.
- Hailing on the Street: If you're outside of a major hotel or area with a taxi stand, you can always hail a taxi directly from the street. When you do, make sure the taxi has the green or red company logo on the side, signaling it's a licensed vehicle. It's a good idea to check the meter immediately after you get in.
- Taxi Apps: For even more convenience, use ride-hailing apps like Grab or GoViet. These apps let you book taxis (or motorbikes) directly from your phone, and they often show you the estimated fare in advance.

How Taxi Fares Are Calculated

Taxis in Hanoi follow a meter system. This means the fare will increase based on the distance traveled, and possibly the time spent stuck in traffic. Here's how the calculation works:

- Flagfall Fee: When you enter the taxi, the meter will start at a fixed fee, usually around 12,000 VND.
- Per-Kilometer Rate: The meter will then charge a set rate per kilometer, typically around 15,000 to 20,000 VND. The total cost increases as you drive further or as traffic slows down.
- Traffic Delays: If there's significant traffic, the meter will also account for the additional time taken to complete the ride, so you'll likely end up paying a little more than if the roads were clear.
- Surcharges: At night or during public holidays, some taxi companies may apply a small surcharge of 10–20%.

It's important to insist on using the meter when getting into a taxi. If the driver suggests a flat rate or seems reluctant to use the meter, it's better to get out and find another taxi.

Recognizing a Licensed Taxi

When hailing a taxi, always make sure it is a licensed vehicle. A licensed taxi in Hanoi will have:

- A company logo (either green for Mai Linh, red for Vinasun, etc.) clearly displayed on the sides of the vehicle.
- A yellow taxi sign on the roof.
- A valid taxi permit (look for the identification number and official license displayed inside the car).
- A taxi meter visibly mounted on the dashboard. This is essential, and if the meter is not in use, you should question the fare.

Taxi Validation for Visitors

Most taxi drivers in Hanoi will speak basic English, but it's helpful to know a few key phrases or have your destination written down in Vietnamese. If you're traveling to a more remote area, it's recommended to have your hotel address or destination in writing. The more you communicate clearly, the smoother the ride will be.

- "How much to [destination]?" – Bao nhiêu đến [địa chỉ]?
- "Please turn on the meter." – Vui lòng bật đồng hồ tính tiền.

Language Tips for Visitors

While many drivers will understand a few key phrases in English, Hanoi's street vendors and taxi drivers are not fluent in the language. It's always good to have your hotel address written in Vietnamese to show the driver or use a translation app like Google Translate if needed. Most major taxi companies have English-speaking drivers, but this might not always be the case with smaller companies.

Final Thoughts

Taxis in Hanoi are convenient and reliable for getting around the city, but understanding how the fare system works and how to recognize a licensed vehicle is crucial for a smooth experience. While other transport options like motorbikes and public transit are also popular, taxis offer a comfortable, air-conditioned way to explore the city. Just remember to always use the meter, know your destination, and enjoy the ride. Whether you're heading to a restaurant, a museum, or a shopping district, taxis provide an efficient way to see the best of Hanoi.

3. First Impressions: Settling into the City

Arriving in Hanoi is like stepping into a whirlwind of sights, sounds, and smells. The city can feel overwhelming at first, but there's a rhythm to it—an energy that quickly pulls you in. As you leave the airport or train station, you'll notice the air is thick with humidity, the hustle of motorbikes weaving through traffic, and the constant hum of life that fills every corner of this vibrant capital.

One of the first things you'll likely notice is the contrast between the old and the new. The Old Quarter is a maze of narrow streets lined with colonial buildings, street vendors, and tiny shops selling everything from fragrant herbs to traditional silk garments. The modern downtown area, however, has sleek high-rises, shopping malls, and cafes where locals and visitors alike gather for coffee or a bite to eat. It's this blend of ancient charm and contemporary urban living that makes Hanoi feel alive with possibility.

Settling in requires a bit of patience. The city's pace is fast, but the locals are friendly and often willing to help if you need directions. Don't be afraid to ask, even if your Vietnamese is limited—many people in Hanoi have a basic understanding of English, especially in tourist-heavy areas.

As you move around, you'll get used to the constant flow of people and vehicles. The motorbikes rule the roads, creating a dance of traffic that seems chaotic yet somehow always finds a way to keep moving. Crossing the street can feel like an adventure in itself, but it's part of the Hanoi experience. The trick? Walk slowly and steadily, and the traffic will move around you.

In these first few days, you'll start to sense what makes Hanoi so special. The city's charm lies in its contrasts, its ability to simultaneously feel both chaotic and peaceful, ancient and modern. You'll soon feel at home, swept up in its pulse, ready to explore everything it has to offer.

4. Staying Safe: Travel Insurance, Emergency Numbers, and Local Laws

While Hanoi is a safe city for travelers, it's always wise to be prepared for the unexpected. From health issues to accidents, having the right information and precautions in place can make your stay much smoother. Here's a quick overview to help you stay safe and protected during your time in the Vietnamese capital.

Travel Insurance

Before you travel, securing comprehensive travel insurance is highly recommended. It covers a variety of scenarios, including medical emergencies, lost luggage, or flight cancellations. Ensure your insurance plan provides coverage for health care and medical evacuation, especially if you're planning to explore remote areas. International insurance providers like World Nomads, Allianz, and Travel Guard offer flexible plans suitable for travelers in Vietnam.

Emergency Numbers

In the event of an emergency, it's crucial to have local emergency numbers on hand. In Hanoi, you can reach the police by dialing 113, fire services are available at 114, and ambulance services can be reached by calling 115. Having these numbers stored in your phone can be a lifesaver in critical situations.

Local Laws and Customs

Vietnamese laws are generally straightforward, but it's important to be aware of some key rules and customs. The legal drinking age is 18, and while alcohol consumption in public is common, excessive drinking or disorderly behavior is not tolerated. Hanoi's roads can be hectic, so always exercise caution when crossing streets, as traffic rules may not be strictly adhered to. Traffic violations can result in fines, especially for things like jaywalking or riding without a helmet on a motorbike.

Vietnam also has strict drug laws. Possession or trafficking of illegal substances can result in severe penalties, including long prison sentences or worse. Additionally, public displays of affection are generally frowned upon in certain parts of Vietnam, so always be mindful of local sensibilities.

By taking some basic precautions, understanding local rules, and having insurance in place, you can feel confident and secure as you enjoy all that Hanoi has to offer.

CHAPTER 2

Iconic Hanoi – Must-See Attractions

Hanoi is a city where history, culture, and legends intertwine. From the serene Hoan Kiem Lake to the bustling Old Quarter, each attraction offers a unique glimpse into the past. Explore Vietnam's heritage at the Temple of Literature and pay respects at the Ho Chi Minh Mausoleum—iconic sights that define the city.

Hoan Kiem Lake: Legends and Landmarks

Location: Hoan Kiem Lake, Hanoi, Vietnam
Address: Hoan Kiem District, Hanoi
GPS: 21.0285° N, 105.8542° E
Opening Hours: Open daily, 24 hours
Admission: Free

Hoan Kiem Lake, or the "Lake of the Restored Sword," holds both natural beauty and a rich cultural significance for Hanoi. Set in the heart of the city, this tranquil body of water is surrounded by a blend of historical landmarks, lush gardens, and the bustling streets of Hanoi's Old Quarter. This picturesque lake is a must-see for anyone visiting the city, offering a peaceful escape from the vibrant urban energy.

History and Legends

Hoan Kiem Lake's legendary status is rooted in Vietnamese folklore. According to local legend, in the 15th century, King Le Loi was gifted a magical sword by the golden turtle of the lake. After using the sword to defeat foreign invaders, the king returned the sword to the turtle, casting it back into the waters—hence the name "Restored Sword." Today, the lake and its surroundings symbolize peace, bravery, and the spirit of Vietnam's independence.

Why Visit?

Beyond its historical significance, Hoan Kiem Lake is the perfect spot to enjoy the harmony of nature and city life. Take a leisurely stroll around the lake, enjoy the serenity of the water, and witness locals practicing tai chi or walking along the tree-lined paths. The lake is an essential stop for any traveler looking to connect with the city's soul.

How to Get There

Hoan Kiem Lake is centrally located and accessible from most points in Hanoi. It's just a short walk from the Old

Quarter. Taxis and motorbike taxis are widely available throughout the city. If you're coming by public transport, Bus No. 09 stops near the lake.

Best Time to Visit

The best time to visit is early morning or late afternoon when the weather is cooler and the lake is less crowded. Sunrise is particularly enchanting, with the soft light reflecting off the water and the peaceful morning activities of Hanoi's residents.

Nearby Attractions

- Ngoc Son Temple: Situated on an island in the lake, this temple is dedicated to the legendary general Tran Hung Dao.
- The Huc Bridge: A beautiful red bridge leading to Ngoc Son Temple, offering a perfect photo opportunity.
- Old Quarter: Just a short walk away, the Old Quarter offers a maze of narrow streets filled with local shops, eateries, and markets.

Photography Tips

The lake provides a great setting for both daytime and evening photography. The reflection of the bridge and surrounding buildings on the water creates beautiful images. For a unique shot, visit at sunrise when the light is soft and the area is quieter.

Practical Information and Rules
- No swimming allowed in the lake.
- Visitors should be respectful of the local customs, particularly when visiting religious sites around the lake.
- While the area is generally safe, be cautious of traffic, especially if crossing roads near the lake.

Nearby Restaurants
- Café Pho Co: A charming café with a view of the lake, offering traditional Vietnamese coffee.
- Quan An Ngon: A popular spot for authentic Vietnamese cuisine, located just a short walk from the lake.

Interesting Facts
- Hoan Kiem Lake is home to the rare and endangered golden turtle, which is said to still reside in the waters.
- The lake and its surrounding areas have long been a gathering place for locals, providing a central meeting point for the people of Hanoi.

For visitors to Hanoi, a trip to Hoan Kiem Lake is more than just sightseeing—it's a chance to experience a blend of natural beauty, cultural heritage, and the city's living history.

2. The Old Quarter: A Walk Through History

Location: Old Quarter, Hanoi, Vietnam
Address: Hoan Kiem District, Hanoi
GPS: 21.0285° N, 105.8542° E
Opening Hours: Open daily, 24 hours
Admission: Free

Hanoi's Old Quarter is the beating pulse of the city, where modern life meets centuries-old history. Located in the heart of Hanoi, this area has been the city's commercial center for over a thousand years. It's here that the streets, each named after the trades once practiced there, form a patchwork of cultural and historical significance.

History and Why Visit

The Old Quarter was originally developed in the 11th century as a merchant hub. Known as "36 Streets," it housed skilled artisans and tradespeople—blacksmiths, silversmiths, and silk makers—who set up shop in the narrow alleys. Today, while the trades have evolved, the character of the neighborhood remains. The Old Quarter is a living museum, with colonial French architecture mingling with Vietnamese heritage.

Visitors are drawn to the area's labyrinthine streets, where small shops and bustling markets line the roads, offering an authentic glimpse into Hanoi's daily life. Whether you're wandering through the busy streets or stopping for a coffee at one of the many cafés, the Old Quarter offers a sensory overload of sights, sounds, and smells.

Best Time to Visit

The best time to visit is early morning or late afternoon, as the streets can get crowded. Morning is especially lovely when vendors set up their stalls, and the area feels quieter. Evening brings a different charm, with neon lights illuminating the streets and the air filled with the scent of street food.

How to Get There

The Old Quarter is centrally located and easily accessible by foot from Hoan Kiem Lake, just a short walk away.

Alternatively, taxis, motorbike taxis, and buses are available throughout the city.

Nearby Attractions
- Hoan Kiem Lake: Just a short walk from the Old Quarter, perfect for a peaceful break.
- Ngoc Son Temple: A serene temple located on an island in Hoan Kiem Lake.
- St. Joseph's Cathedral: A beautiful piece of French colonial architecture located on Nha Tho Street.

Photography Tips

The narrow streets, old buildings, and vibrant markets make for great photography opportunities. Early morning light casts a warm glow over the scene, and the chaotic beauty of the street markets is perfect for capturing the essence of Hanoi.

Practical Information
- The Old Quarter is open 24 hours a day, but the best time to explore is during daylight hours when the area is lively.
- The streets can be crowded, so be prepared for a bit of noise and hustle.

- Be mindful of traffic when crossing the road; it's always a bit chaotic.

Interesting Facts
- The Old Quarter's 36 streets were originally named for the craft practiced there, such as Hang Bac (Silver Street) and Hang Duong (Sugar Street).
- The Old Quarter is home to some of Hanoi's best street food, with numerous food stalls offering local specialties like pho and bun cha.

The Old Quarter offers an immersive step back in time and a vibrant snapshot of Hanoi's present-day culture. It's where history, local life, and modernity blend seamlessly, creating an experience unlike any other.

3. Ho Chi Minh Mausoleum and Museum

Location: Ho Chi Minh Mausoleum
Address: 2 Hung Vuong, Dien Bien, Ba Dinh, Hanoi, Vietnam
GPS: 21.0367° N, 105.8342° E
Official Website: http://www.baotanghochiminh.vn)
Opening Hours:

- Mausoleum: Daily (except Mondays and Fridays), 7:30 AM – 10:30 AM
- Museum: Daily, 8:00 AM – 11:00 AM and 2:00 PM – 4:30 PM
- Admission: Free for the Mausoleum; Museum: VND 25,000 (Approx. $1)

Overview and History

The Ho Chi Minh Mausoleum is one of Hanoi's most significant landmarks and a must-see for anyone visiting the city. The Mausoleum is the final resting place of Vietnam's beloved leader, Ho Chi Minh, who played a central role in the country's fight for independence. Built in 1973 and modeled after Lenin's Mausoleum in Moscow, this imposing structure is a symbol of Ho Chi Minh's legacy and Vietnam's revolutionary history.

The mausoleum itself is a solemn place of respect, where the embalmed body of Ho Chi Minh lies in state. The building is surrounded by lush gardens, and while the structure is modern, it exudes a quiet reverence.

Why You Should Visit

Visiting the Mausoleum offers an emotional experience, allowing visitors to reflect on Vietnam's path to independence while paying homage to one of its most revered leaders. The nearby Ho Chi Minh Museum adds further depth, offering a closer look at his life and the key events that shaped the nation.

How to Get There

Located in Hanoi's Ba Dinh District, the Mausoleum is easily accessible by taxi, motorbike, or bus. From Hoan Kiem Lake, it's a short 15-minute ride by car or motorbike. You can also walk, which will take about 30 minutes.

Nearby Attractions and Things to Do

- Presidential Palace: Just a short walk from the Mausoleum, this French colonial building was once the home of Vietnam's rulers.
- One Pillar Pagoda: Located nearby, this historic pagoda is built atop a single stone pillar in the middle of a pond.
- Ho Chi Minh Museum: This museum is dedicated to Ho Chi Minh's life and legacy, showcasing exhibits that narrate Vietnam's struggle for independence.

Best Time to Visit

It's best to visit early in the morning to avoid the crowds. The Mausoleum is busiest on weekends, so weekdays tend to be more peaceful.

Photography Tips

Photography is prohibited inside the Mausoleum, but you can take photos of the exterior and surrounding gardens. The light in the morning is perfect for capturing the impressive structure.

Practical Information and Laws/Rules

- Dress Code: Visitors are required to dress modestly when entering the Mausoleum. Sleeveless tops, shorts, and skirts above the knee are not allowed.
- Behavior: The Mausoleum is a solemn site. Visitors should remain quiet and respectful.
- Security: Bags are not allowed inside, and you will be required to pass through security checks.

4. Temple of Literature: Exploring Vietnam's Heritage

Location: Temple of Literature

Address: 58 Quoc Tu Giam Street, Dong Da, Hanoi, Vietnam

GPS: 21.0275° N, 105.8342° E
Official Website: http://www.vhttdlhanoi.gov.vn)
Opening Hours:
Daily: 8:00 AM – 5:00 PM
Admission: VND 30,000 (Approx. $1.30)

Overview and History

The Temple of Literature (Văn Miếu), built in 1070 during the reign of Emperor Ly Thanh Tong, is one of Hanoi's oldest and most revered sites. Initially constructed to honor Confucius, the temple became a national center for education and housed Vietnam's first university. It was a place where scholars gathered to study and take exams for the imperial court. Today, the Temple of Literature stands as a symbol of Vietnam's deep respect for education, culture, and intellectual achievement.

This serene and picturesque site is a must-visit for anyone wanting to connect with the ancient roots of Vietnamese scholarship. The complex is composed of five courtyards, each one more tranquil and beautiful than the last, filled with statues, steles, and lush greenery.

Why You Should Visit

Beyond its historical significance, the Temple offers a peaceful retreat from the hustle of Hanoi's busy streets. Its traditional architecture and well-maintained gardens provide a calm space for reflection. Visitors can explore the intricate carvings and the famous stelae (stone tablets) inscribed with the names of successful graduates from the imperial examinations. For history lovers and those interested in Vietnam's educational heritage, this site is a rich and rewarding visit.

How to Get There

Located in Hanoi's Dong Da District, the Temple of Literature is easily reachable by taxi, motorbike, or bus from the city center. It's about a 10-minute ride from Hoan Kiem Lake and easily accessible by foot from other nearby landmarks.

Best Time to Visit

The Temple is open year-round, but the best time to visit is early in the morning when the air is cool and the crowds are thinner. Weekdays are less crowded compared to weekends.

Nearby Attractions and Things to Do
- Hoan Kiem Lake: Just a short drive away, the lake offers a lovely spot to relax and people-watch.
- Vietnam Fine Arts Museum: A 15-minute walk from the Temple, this museum displays an impressive collection of Vietnamese art.
- One Pillar Pagoda: A historic pagoda built in 1049, located nearby, known for its unique design.

Photography Tips
The Temple's courtyards, serene ponds, and statues make for fantastic photos. Early morning light creates a soft, golden glow over the complex, ideal for capturing the intricate architectural details and quiet ambiance. Be mindful of other visitors when taking pictures.

Practical Information and Laws/Rules
- Dress Code: Modest clothing is required—no sleeveless tops or shorts above the knee.
- Behavior: Keep noise levels low as the temple is a place of reverence.
- Security: Security checks are in place, so bags are subject to inspection.

CHAPTER 3

Accommodation Options for Every Traveler

Hanoi offers accommodation for every type of traveler, from luxurious resorts to budget-friendly hostels. Whether you're seeking a lavish stay, a cozy guesthouse, or a cultural experience in a homestay, the city caters to all. Explore the best neighborhoods, from the bustling Old Quarter to the serene Tay Ho area.

1. Luxury Stays: Hanoi's Top-Rated Hotels and Resorts

1. Sofitel Legend Metropole Hanoi

Address: 15 Ngo Quyen Street, Hanoi, Vietnam

GPS: 21.0337° N, 105.8540° E

Website: https://www.sofitel-legend-metropole-hanoi.com)

A historical icon in the heart of Hanoi, Sofitel Legend Metropole Hanoi blends French colonial elegance with modern luxury. Established in 1901, the property offers refined rooms, high-end dining, and exceptional service, making it a favorite among travelers seeking a lavish stay.

The hotel features two outdoor pools, a fitness center, a spa, and multiple dining options.

Room Features & Types
Rooms vary from classic French-style suites to spacious Opera Wing rooms with modern touches. Highlights include marble bathrooms, deep soaking tubs, and plush bedding.

- Deluxe Rooms: Ideal for couples or solo travelers looking for comfort and style.
- Grand Luxury Suites: Perfect for those desiring a more spacious and opulent stay, with access to exclusive services.

Advantages
- Close proximity to the Old Quarter and key attractions like Hoan Kiem Lake and the Opera House.
- Impeccable service with a focus on detail.
- Historical significance adds an immersive cultural experience.

Disadvantages
- Price range may be high for budget-conscious travelers.
- Rooms on the lower floors may experience street noise.

How to Get There

From Noi Bai International Airport: Approximately 45 minutes by car (30 km). Taxis are readily available, or you can arrange a pick-up through the hotel.

Directions

Located in central Hanoi, it's a 5-minute walk from Hoan Kiem Lake, and 10 minutes from the famous Hanoi Opera House.

Price Range

$200 - $500 per night, depending on room type and season.

Contact Information

Tel: +84 24 3826 6919

Email: h1515@sofitel.com

2. InterContinental Hanoi Westlake

Address: 5 Tu Hoa Street, Tay Ho District, Hanoi, Vietnam

GPS: 21.0621° N, 105.8493° E

Website: (https://www.ihg.com/intercontinental/hotels/us/en/hanoi/hanhb/hoteldetail)

This luxurious lakeside retreat is set on Hanoi's West Lake, offering serene views and an array of high-end amenities. The InterContinental Hanoi Westlake combines comfort, convenience, and elegance, with spacious rooms, a full-service spa, and a variety of dining options. Guests can unwind by the outdoor pool or explore the nearby attractions.

Room Features & Types
- Superior Rooms: Beautifully decorated with expansive views of West Lake.
- Lakeview Suites: Perfect for those who want a private balcony and more space.
- Villas: Luxurious, standalone accommodations ideal for families or long stays.

Advantages
- Peaceful lakeside setting, a short distance from Hanoi's vibrant city center.
- Well-equipped for both business and leisure stays.

Disadvantages
- Distance from central attractions may require taxis or a longer walk.
- Can feel isolated for travelers looking for direct access to bustling city life.

How to Get There

From Noi Bai International Airport: About 45 minutes by car (25 km). Taxis or private hotel transfers are recommended.

Directions

Located near the West Lake, 15 minutes by taxi to Hoan Kiem Lake, Hanoi's center.

Price Range

$150 - $350 per night.

Contact Information

Tel: +84 24 6270 8888

Email: ic.hanoi@ihg.com

3. Hanoi La Siesta Hotel & Spa

Address: 94 Ma May Street, Old Quarter, Hanoi, Vietnam

GPS: 21.0312° N, 105.8543° E

Website: https://www.hanoilasiestahotel.com)

Set in the lively Old Quarter, this upscale boutique hotel combines luxury with a personalized touch. With its cozy interiors and tranquil spa services, it's an excellent choice for those who want a premium stay without being too far from the action. The property is known for its excellent customer service and elegantly designed rooms.

Room Features & Types

- Deluxe Rooms: Bright and contemporary, with views of the Old Quarter.
- Premier Rooms: Slightly larger, offering enhanced amenities and decor.

Advantages

- Located in the heart of Hanoi's Old Quarter, perfect for shopping and sightseeing.
- Excellent spa services and well-regarded dining.

Disadvantages

- Can be noisy given its location in a busy area.
- Rooms may feel smaller compared to other luxury hotels.

How to Get There

From Noi Bai International Airport: About 45 minutes by car (30 km). A taxi ride costs around $15.

Directions

Situated in Hanoi's Old Quarter, walking distance to Hoan Kiem Lake and the Night Market.

Price Range

$120 - $250 per night.

Contact Information

Tel: +84 24 3928 3848

Email: info@hanoilasiestahotel.com

4. Lotte Hotel Hanoi

Address: 54 Lieu Giai Street, Ba Dinh District, Hanoi, Vietnam

GPS: 21.0370° N, 105.8349° E

Website: (https://www.lottehotel.com/hanoi-hotel/en.html)

Located in Hanoi's central business district, Lotte Hotel combines luxury with convenience. Its top floors provide stunning panoramic views of the city, and guests can enjoy a range of fine dining and wellness options. The hotel is part of a larger complex that includes shopping malls and offices, offering plenty of entertainment options nearby.

Room Features & Types
- Superior Rooms: Elegant, with views of the city.
- Executive Suites: Larger with added benefits such as access to the executive lounge.

Advantages
- Great location for both business and leisure travelers.
- Excellent views of Hanoi and West Lake from upper floors.

Disadvantages
- Price range is higher, making it less accessible for budget travelers.
- Not as close to the main tourist attractions as other luxury hotels.

How to Get There
From Noi Bai International Airport: Approximately 40 minutes by car (26 km).

Directions
Located in the business district, a 10-minute drive to the Old Quarter.

Price Range
$180 - $400 per night.

Contact Information
Tel: +84 24 3333 1000
Email: hanoi@lotte.net

2. Budget-Friendly Choices: Hostels and Guesthouses

Hanoi's affordable hostels and guesthouses offer an authentic, no-frills experience for budget travelers. Whether you're a backpacker or just seeking to stretch your travel budget, these accommodations provide comfort, convenience, and a great base for exploring the city.

1. Hanoi Backpackers Hostel
Address: 9 Ma May Street, Hoan Kiem District, Hanoi, Vietnam
Estimated Budget: $8 - $15 per night for a dorm bed, $20 - $35 for a private room
A popular choice among young travelers, Hanoi Backpackers Hostel offers a vibrant atmosphere with nightly events like pub crawls and social gatherings. It's located in the Old Quarter, making it easy to explore local attractions on foot. The hostel provides free Wi-Fi, a bar, and a tour

desk to help with sightseeing plans. If you're looking to meet fellow travelers, this is the place.

2. Little Hanoi Hostel

Address: 30 Hang Ga Street, Hoan Kiem District, Hanoi, Vietnam

Estimated Budget: $10 - $18 per night for a dorm bed, $25 - $45 for a private room

Little Hanoi Hostel is a small, welcoming spot with a homely vibe. Situated near the bustling Old Quarter, this hostel makes it easy to explore Hanoi's lively streets. Free breakfast, Wi-Fi, and coffee are included, and staff are always eager to share tips on where to eat and what to see. The private rooms are cozy, making it a solid choice for those wanting more privacy without breaking the bank.

3. Hanoi Guesthouse

Address: 70 Ma May Street, Hoan Kiem District, Hanoi, Vietnam

Estimated Budget: $12 - $25 per night for a dorm bed, $30 - $50 for a private room

Hanoi Guesthouse is a family-run establishment known for its warm hospitality and comfortable rooms. Located in the heart of the Old Quarter, it's just a short walk to Hoan Kiem

Lake and local attractions. The guesthouse offers air-conditioned rooms, free breakfast, and excellent service. It's perfect for those who want a quiet, affordable stay with easy access to Hanoi's main sights.

4. The Signature Inn

Address: 22 Bat Dan Street, Hoan Kiem District, Hanoi, Vietnam

Estimated Budget: $15 - $25 per night for a dorm bed, $30 - $60 for a private room

The Signature Inn combines budget-friendly prices with a high level of service. Located near the Old Quarter, it's an ideal spot for travelers looking for a peaceful stay. Rooms are modern, and the guesthouse offers free breakfast, Wi-Fi, and assistance with arranging tours. It's known for being a comfortable, low-cost option for those who want to enjoy Hanoi without the hefty price tag.

Getting Around

Most of these budget accommodations are within walking distance of key attractions like the Hoan Kiem Lake, the Hanoi Opera House, and the Night Market. For longer trips, taxis and Grab (Southeast Asia's ride-sharing service) are affordable and convenient.

Conclusion

For the budget-conscious traveler, Hanoi's hostels and guesthouses offer a variety of options. Whether you're looking for a social atmosphere or a quiet retreat, you'll find something that suits your needs, all without stretching your budget.

3. Boutique Hotels and Homestays: A Cultural Experience

Hanoi's boutique hotels and homestays offer a blend of comfort, local charm, and authentic Vietnamese experiences. These accommodations allow visitors to immerse themselves in the culture of this vibrant city, all while enjoying personalized service and a homely atmosphere.

1. The Hanoi Club Hotel & Lake Palais Residences
Address: 76 Yen Phu Street, Tay Ho District, Hanoi, Vietnam
GPS: 21.0426° N, 105.8540° E
Official Website: http://www.hanoiclubhotel.com.vn)
Price Range: $60 - $120 per night

Description:

Located on the edge of West Lake, The Hanoi Club Hotel blends colonial-style architecture with modern amenities. With spacious rooms overlooking the lake, it offers a serene environment for travelers looking for peace and luxury. The property is known for its excellent dining options, outdoor pool, and wellness center.

Amenities:
- Free Wi-Fi
- Fitness center
- Outdoor pool
- On-site restaurant and bar
- Full-service spa

Room Features:
- Air conditioning
- Flat-screen TV
- Mini bar
- Private balcony with lake views
- En-suite bathroom with a shower and bathtub

Advantages:
- Tranquil lakeside location
- High-end facilities

- Great dining options

Disadvantages:

- Slightly removed from Hanoi's central attractions (20-minute drive)

How to Get There:
From Noi Bai International Airport (30 minutes by car).
Contact: +84 24 3823 9360

2. Hanoi La Siesta Hotel & Spa
Address: 94 Ma May Street, Hoan Kiem District, Hanoi, Vietnam
GPS: 21.0322° N, 105.8546° E
Official Website: https://www.lasiestahotels.com
Price Range: $50 - $90 per night

Description:
This stylish boutique hotel in the Old Quarter is known for its sleek design and exceptional service. Hanoi La Siesta is a blend of modern luxury and traditional charm, offering guests an intimate, yet high-end stay. The on-site spa and restaurant are highlights.

Amenities:
- Free Wi-Fi
- Fitness center
- Spa and wellness center
- On-site restaurant serving Vietnamese cuisine

Room Features:
- King-sized beds
- Smart TV
- Minibar
- Luxurious bathrobes and slippers

Advantages:
- Perfect location in the Old Quarter
- Highly rated spa services
- Cozy, boutique feel

Disadvantages:
- Limited views, as it's located in a bustling part of the city

How to Get There:
From Noi Bai International Airport, take a taxi (30 minutes).
Contact: +84 24 3935 2255

3. Hanoi Street View Hostel & Homestay

Address: 13 Hang Buom Street, Hoan Kiem District, Hanoi, Vietnam

GPS: 21.0335° N, 105.8563° E

Official Website: http://www.hanoistreetviewhostel.com)

Price Range: $25 - $60 per night

Description:

For those looking for a homestay experience, Hanoi Street View is a small family-run guesthouse that feels more like staying with friends than at a hotel. It offers clean, simple rooms with local flair and is conveniently located near major attractions in Hanoi.

Amenities:
- Free Wi-Fi
- 24-hour front desk
- Shared kitchen
- Bicycle rentals

Room Features:
- Comfortable beds
- Air conditioning
- Shared or private bathrooms
- Advantages:

- Authentic local experience
- Affordable for solo travelers or small groups

Disadvantages:

- Limited luxury amenities
- Shared bathrooms may not be ideal for everyone

How to Get There:

From Noi Bai International Airport, take a taxi (35 minutes).

Contact: +84 24 3935 6620

4. The Old Quarter View Hanoi Hostel

Address: 45 Hang Ma Street, Hoan Kiem District, Hanoi, Vietnam

GPS: 21.0342° N, 105.8550° E

Official Website: https://www.oldquarterviewhanoi.com

Price Range: $15 - $40 per night

Description:

This cozy homestay offers a warm, traditional feel with modern touches. Located in the bustling Old Quarter, it gives guests a chance to experience Hanoi's culture up close. The hotel offers both dormitory-style and private rooms, making it an excellent choice for budget-conscious travelers.

Amenities:

- Free Wi-Fi
- Free breakfast
- Airport transfer service
- Tour desk

Room Features:

- Basic furnishings
- Comfortable bedding
- Air conditioning
- Private or shared bathrooms

Advantages:

- Central location for sightseeing
- Great value for money

Disadvantages:

- Can be noisy due to proximity to the Old Quarter

How to Get There:

From the airport, it's a 40-minute drive by taxi.

Contact: +84 24 3928 4108

These boutique hotels and homestays provide travelers with affordable and authentic experiences that connect them with the culture of Hanoi. From modern amenities to homely comforts, these places offer a personalized touch that larger hotels often miss.

4. Choosing the Right Neighborhood: Old Quarter, Tay Ho, and Beyond

When planning your stay in Hanoi, the choice of neighborhood plays a key role in shaping your experience. Each district offers a distinct atmosphere, making it essential to pick the one that aligns with your preferences. Here's a closer look at the main neighborhoods for visitors.

1. Old Quarter (Hoan Kiem District)

Description:

The Old Quarter is the beating heart of Hanoi. This historic area is famous for its narrow, winding streets, vibrant markets, and colonial architecture. Here, you'll find a blend of traditional Vietnamese life with modern influences, making it a top choice for first-time visitors. It's where you can truly experience the city's charm.

Amenities:

- Proximity to major attractions like Hoan Kiem Lake and the Hanoi Opera House

- Numerous cafes, shops, and street food stalls
- Excellent public transportation connections

Advantages:
- Central location, ideal for sightseeing
- High energy and vibrant street life
- Walking distance to most attractions

Disadvantages:
- Can be crowded and noisy
- Accommodations range from budget to mid-range; luxury options are limited

How to Get There:
From Noi Bai International Airport (45 minutes by taxi or ride-hailing app).
Price Range: Budget to mid-range, $30 - $100 per night.
Contact: Varies by accommodation choice

2. Tay Ho (West Lake District)
Description:
Tay Ho is a peaceful lakeside district located a bit further from Hanoi's historical center. It's known for its spacious atmosphere, making it a great choice for travelers seeking a more relaxed environment. West Lake, one of Hanoi's

largest bodies of water, provides a beautiful backdrop for upscale hotels, restaurants, and expat communities.

Amenities:
- Scenic lakeside views
- Quiet, residential feel with plenty of green spaces
- Boutique shopping and fine dining options

Advantages:
- Peaceful and less chaotic than the Old Quarter
- Large number of high-end hotels and international restaurants
- Ideal for families or long-term stays

Disadvantages:
- Farther from the main tourist spots (20-30 minutes by taxi)
- Fewer local markets and street food stalls

How to Get There:
From the airport, take a taxi (40-minute drive).
Price Range: Mid-range to luxury, $50 - $150 per night.
Contact: Varies by accommodation choice

3. Ba Dinh District

Description:

Ba Dinh is a quieter, more residential area that offers a blend of history and culture. It's home to iconic landmarks like the Ho Chi Minh Mausoleum and the Presidential Palace. This district is ideal for history buffs and those who prefer a slower pace without being far from key attractions.

Amenities:
- Close to cultural landmarks
- Calm and relaxed environment
- Local Vietnamese cafes and eateries

Advantages:
- Close to cultural attractions
- Less crowded than the Old Quarter
- More authentic local experiences

Disadvantages:
- More residential, fewer hotels and nightlife options
- Can be quieter in the evenings

How to Get There:

From the airport, take a taxi (35-minute drive).

Price Range: Budget to mid-range, $30 - $80 per night.

Contact: Varies by accommodation choice

4. Hai Ba Trung District

Description:

Hai Ba Trung is a commercial district with a vibrant mix of shopping, dining, and entertainment. It offers a good balance of modern amenities and local experiences. It's an excellent choice for travelers looking for a local experience but who also appreciate convenience.

Amenities:
- Easy access to shopping malls and restaurants
- Quiet residential areas
- Good mix of hotels and guesthouses

Advantages:
- Central location, close to shopping and restaurants
- Quieter than the Old Quarter
- Great for longer stays due to local feel

Disadvantages:
- More commercial, less focused on tourism
- Not as many traditional sights

How to Get There:

From the airport, take a taxi (40 minutes).

Price Range: Mid-range to luxury, $40 - $120 per night.

Contact: Varies by accommodation choice

Which Neighborhood Should You Choose?

- Old Quarter is the perfect choice if you want to be in the center of Hanoi's energy and close to historical landmarks.
- Tay Ho offers a peaceful lakeside retreat with luxury options and a more relaxed vibe.
- Ba Dinh is ideal for history lovers who prefer quiet residential streets.
- Hai Ba Trung strikes a balance between local life and convenience, with easy access to shopping and dining.

Each neighborhood provides a different slice of Hanoi, and your choice should depend on your personal travel style.

CHAPTER 4

A Taste of Hanoi – Food and Drink

Hanoi's food scene is a journey in itself. From the world-famous Pho to the lesser-known street foods, the city's culinary delights are sure to excite every palate. Whether you're tasting iconic dishes, sipping unique beverages like egg coffee, or learning through food tours, Hanoi offers unforgettable dining experiences at every corner.

1. Hanoi's Iconic Dishes: Pho, Bun Cha, and Beyond

Hanoi, Vietnam's capital, is famous for its food culture, which reflects a mix of history, tradition, and authentic flavors. Here's a guide to four must-try dishes that define Hanoi's culinary landscape.

1. Pho

Description: Pho is Vietnam's signature noodle soup, featuring a rich, aromatic broth made from simmered bones, star anise, and cinnamon. It's served with soft rice noodles, tender slices of beef or chicken, and fresh herbs.

Location: Pho Gia Truyen Bat Dan
Address: 49 Bat Dan, Hoan Kiem District, Hanoi
GPS: 21.0355° N, 105.8459° E
Contact: +84 24 6686 8149

- What to Eat and Drink: Try the beef pho (pho bo) with a side of lime and chili for an extra kick. Pair it with iced tea or fresh lime juice.
- Estimated Fees: $2.50 - $3.50 per bowl.
- Payment Options: Cash only.

2. Bun Cha

Description: A flavorful dish of grilled pork patties and slices, served in a tangy-sweet fish sauce broth alongside fresh herbs and vermicelli noodles.

Location: Bun Cha Huong Lien
Address: 24 Le Van Huu, Hai Ba Trung District, Hanoi
GPS: 21.0142° N, 105.8482° E
Contact: +84 24 3943 4106

What to Eat and Drink: Opt for the classic bun cha set and pair it with fresh spring rolls. For drinks, try Vietnamese iced coffee or fresh coconut water.

Estimated Fees: $3 - $4 per set.

Payment Options: Cash and local e-wallets.

3. Cha Ca

Description: Cha Ca is grilled fish marinated with turmeric and spices, served with dill, peanuts, rice noodles, and fish sauce.

Location: Cha Ca Thang Long

Address: 19-21-31 Duong Thanh, Hoan Kiem District, Hanoi

GPS: 21.0296° N, 105.8472° E

Contact: +84 24 3828 7207

What to Eat and Drink: Enjoy the signature cha ca with noodles and herbs, accompanied by a cold local beer.

Estimated Fees: $6 - $8 per portion.

Payment Options: Cash, cards, and e-wallets.

4. Banh Mi

Description: This Vietnamese sandwich combines a crispy baguette with fillings like pork, pate, pickled vegetables, and fresh cilantro.

Location: Banh Mi 25

Address: 25 Hang Ca, Hoan Kiem District, Hanoi

GPS: 21.0383° N, 105.8470° E

Contact: +84 97 766 8786

Website: http://banhmi25.com)

- What to Eat and Drink: Try the classic pork banh mi or vegetarian option. Pair with fresh fruit juice.
- Estimated Fees: $1.50 - $2.50 per sandwich.
- Payment Options: Cash, cards, and e-wallets.

Each of these dishes represents Hanoi's vibrant food culture, making your visit unforgettable and flavorful.

2. Best Street Food Spots: Hidden Gems and Famous Eateries

Hanoi is a paradise for street food lovers, offering vibrant flavors and dishes steeped in tradition. Here's a guide to five must-try street foods, their highlights, where to find them, and how to enjoy them.

1. Pho

Dish Description: Pho is a fragrant noodle soup made with a clear, savory broth, flat rice noodles, and slices of beef or chicken. Fresh herbs, lime, and chili enhance its layers of flavor.
- Price Range: $2 - $3 per bowl.
- Where to Find It:

1. Pho Gia Truyen Bat Dan: 49 Bat Dan Street (GPS: 21.0355° N, 105.8459° E).

2. Pho Thin: 13 Lo Duc Street (GPS: 21.0145° N, 105.8563° E).

3. Pho 10 Ly Quoc Su: 10 Ly Quoc Su Street (GPS: 21.0327° N, 105.8482° E).

- Preparation: The broth is slow-cooked with bones, star anise, and cinnamon for depth. Rice noodles are added, topped with thin slices of meat and garnished with herbs.
- Taste Profile: Light and aromatic, with a balance of umami, sweetness, and fresh herbal notes.
- Dining Tip: Typically eaten for breakfast. Locals slurp their pho loudly—it's a sign of enjoyment!

2. Bun Cha

Dish Description: Bun Cha features grilled pork patties and slices served in a tangy fish sauce broth with fresh herbs and vermicelli noodles.

- Price Range: $2.50 - $4 per set.
- Where to Find It:

1. Bun Cha Huong Lien: 24 Le Van Huu Street (GPS: 21.0142° N, 105.8482° E).

2. Bun Cha Dac Kim: 1 Hang Manh Street (GPS: 21.0337° N, 105.8470° E).

3. Bun Cha Sinh Tu: 2 Nguyen Khuyen Street (GPS: 21.0293° N, 105.8376° E).

- Preparation: Pork is marinated and grilled over charcoal. The sauce combines fish sauce, sugar, vinegar, and garlic.
- Taste Profile: Smoky, tangy, and slightly sweet, balanced by the freshness of herbs.
- Dining Tip: Lunch is the best time to eat bun cha, as most vendors sell out by mid-afternoon.

3. Banh Mi

- Dish Description: This Vietnamese sandwich is made with a crispy baguette filled with pork, pate, pickled vegetables, and cilantro.
- Price Range: $1.50 - $2.50.
- Where to Find It:

1. Banh Mi 25: 25 Hang Ca Street (GPS: 21.0383° N, 105.8470° E).

2. Banh Mi Pho Hue: 118 Pho Hue Street (GPS: 21.0128° N, 105.8514° E).

3. Banh Mi Lan Ong: 8 Cha Ca Street (GPS: 21.0367° N, 105.8476° E).

- Preparation: The baguette is lightly toasted, then stuffed with layers of meat, pate, and pickles.

- Taste Profile: Crunchy, tangy, and savory with a hint of spice.
- Dining Tip: Perfect for a quick snack anytime.

4. Xoi (Sticky Rice)
- Dish Description: Sticky rice is served with various toppings like shredded chicken, pork floss, or fried shallots.
- Price Range: $1.50 - $3.
- Where to Find It:

   1. Xoi Yen: 35B Nguyen Huu Huan Street (GPS: 21.0338° N, 105.8500° E).

   2. Xoi May: 99 Nguyen Cong Tru Street (GPS: 21.0150° N, 105.8565° E).

   3. Xoi Ba Thin: 1 Bat Dan Street (GPS: 21.0356° N, 105.8462° E).

- Preparation: Sticky rice is steamed until soft, then topped with savory or sweet additions.
- Taste Profile: Chewy and comforting, with a mix of salty, sweet, and crispy flavors.
- Dining Tip: A popular breakfast choice, but also great for a light dinner.

5. Nem Ran (Spring Rolls)

- Dish Description: Crispy fried spring rolls stuffed with minced pork, mushrooms, glass noodles, and vegetables.
- Price Range: $1 - $1.50 per roll.
- Where to Find It:

1. Quan Goc Da: 52 Ly Quoc Su Street (GPS: 21.0330° N, 105.8480° E).

2. Bun Cha Ta: 21 Hang Than Street (GPS: 21.0410° N, 105.8496° E).

3. Bun Nem: 35 Hang Manh Street (GPS: 21.0340° N, 105.8472° E).

- Preparation: Rolls are deep-fried to golden perfection.
- Taste Profile: Crispy and savory with a flavorful dipping sauce.
- Dining Tip: Often served as a side dish for festive meals.

Etiquette and Phrases

- Locals prefer eating meals fresh, so avoid ordering to-go unless necessary.
- Always say "Cảm ơn" (Thank you) to show politeness.
- Practice "Cho tôi một ..." (Please give me one...) to order dishes confidently.

Street food in Hanoi isn't just a meal; it's an experience rooted in culture and tradition. These hidden gems and famous spots offer an authentic taste of the city.

3. Cafés and Unique Beverages: Egg Coffee and Tea Houses

Hanoi is well-known for its vibrant café culture, which seamlessly blends traditional tastes with modern creativity. Among its standout offerings are the famous egg coffee and the tranquil tea houses that provide an authentic local experience.

Egg Coffee: A Hanoi Specialty

Egg coffee, or "cà phê trứng," is a one-of-a-kind drink created in Hanoi in the 1940s. It combines robust Vietnamese coffee with a frothy, sweet layer of whisked egg yolk, sugar, and condensed milk. The result is a rich, velvety beverage with a custard-like texture, served hot or iced.

Where to Try It:

1. Café Giang: 39 Nguyen Huu Huan Street (GPS: 21.0334° N, 105.8510° E). The birthplace of egg coffee, known for its traditional preparation.

2. Loading T Café: 8 Chan Cam Street (GPS: 21.0321° N, 105.8474° E). A cozy spot in a French colonial building offering a unique take on the classic.

3. Note Coffee: 64 Luong Van Can Street (GPS: 21.0312° N, 105.8501° E). Famous for its colorful, personalized notes left by visitors worldwide.

- Price Range: $2 - $3.
- Taste Profile: Sweet, creamy, and slightly bitter, perfectly balanced with the boldness of Vietnamese coffee.

Tea Houses: A Tradition of Serenity

Hanoi's tea houses offer a quiet escape from the bustling streets. Traditional tea, made with jasmine, lotus, or green tea leaves, is steeped with care and often accompanied by light snacks like mooncakes or sunflower seeds. These tea houses are perfect for unwinding and experiencing Vietnamese hospitality.

Where to Go:

1. Thái Hòa Tea House: 6 Hang Bac Street (GPS: 21.0350° N, 105.8496° E). A serene spot offering a variety of traditional teas.

2. Tranquil Books & Coffee: 5 Nguyen Quang Bich Street (GPS: 21.0347° N, 105.8465° E). Combines a peaceful atmosphere with an excellent selection of teas and books.

3. Ha Thai Tea House: 17D To Ngoc Van Street (GPS: 21.0598° N, 105.8267° E). Known for its lotus tea and tranquil setting.

- Price Range: $1.50 - $4.
- Taste Profile: Fresh, floral, and calming, with subtle sweetness depending on the brew.

Dining Tips
- Egg coffee is best enjoyed slowly, letting the flavors meld with every sip. Use a spoon to mix the frothy egg layer into the coffee for a balanced taste.
- At tea houses, pour tea for others before serving yourself as a sign of respect.

4. Food Tours and Cooking Classes: Learn and Indulge

Hanoi's food scene is a treasure trove for enthusiasts eager to not only taste its iconic dishes but also learn the art of Vietnamese cooking. Here are five food tours and cooking classes that offer an immersive experience, showcasing the flavors and techniques behind Hanoi's most beloved meals.

1. Hanoi Street Food Tour
- Highlights: This walking tour takes you through Hanoi's Old Quarter, where you sample iconic dishes like Pho, Bun Cha, and Banh Cuon.
- Dish Details:
  Pho: A fragrant noodle soup with beef or chicken, fresh herbs, and spices.
  Banh Cuon: Steamed rice rolls stuffed with minced pork and mushrooms.
- Price Range: $25 - $35 per person.
- Where to Book:

1. Hanoi Street Food Tour: 74 Hang Bac Street (GPS: 21.0351° N, 105.8506° E).

2. Old Quarter Foodie Tour: 14 Hang Buom Street (GPS: 21.0363° N, 105.8518° E).

3. Vietnam Awesome Travel: 19B Hang Be Street (GPS: 21.0339° N, 105.8503° E).

- Taste Profile: A mix of savory, spicy, and aromatic flavors from street food staples.
- Dining Tips: Wear comfortable shoes and bring an appetite—you'll be tasting many small dishes.

2. Hidden Hanoi Cooking Class
- Highlights: A hands-on class where you learn to prepare dishes like Nem Ran (spring rolls) and Cha Ca (turmeric grilled fish).
- Dish Details:
  Nem Ran: Crispy spring rolls stuffed with pork, mushrooms, and noodles.
  Cha Ca: Grilled fish marinated in turmeric and served with dill and noodles.
- Price Range: $30 - $45 per class.
- Where to Book:

1. Hidden Hanoi: 147 Nghi Tam Street (GPS: 21.0560° N, 105.8315° E).

2. Apron Up Cooking Class: 74 Hang Bac Street (GPS: 21.0351° N, 105.8506° E).

3. Rose Kitchen Hanoi: 16 Ngoc Ha Street (GPS: 21.0379° N, 105.8352° E).

- Preparation Tips: You'll start with a market tour to gather ingredients before cooking.
- Dining Etiquette: Share dishes family style, a hallmark of Vietnamese dining.

3. Morning Market and Cooking Class

- Highlights: This class begins with a guided visit to a bustling market to learn about local ingredients. You'll prepare dishes like Xoi Ga (sticky rice with chicken) and Pho Ga (chicken pho).
- Dish Details:

  Xoi Ga: Sticky rice topped with shredded chicken and fried shallots.

  Pho Ga: A lighter version of pho with a chicken-based broth.
- Price Range: $30 - $40 per person.

Where to Book:

1. Hanoi Cooking Centre: 44 Chau Long Street (GPS: 21.0417° N, 105.8439° E).

2. Travel and Chef: 6 Le Thai To Street (GPS: 21.0285° N, 105.8507° E).

3. Eco Cooking Class: 32 Dao Duy Tu Street (GPS: 21.0338° N, 105.8524° E).

Cultural Note: Markets are busiest in the early morning, the best time to experience the vibrant atmosphere.

4. Hanoi Vegan Cooking Class

Highlights: Perfect for vegetarians and vegans, this class teaches plant-based versions of Vietnamese dishes like Bun

Rieu Chay (vegetarian noodle soup) and Goi Cuon (fresh spring rolls).

- Price Range: $35 - $50 per class.
- Where to Book:

1. Vegan Zone Hanoi: 18 Phan Chu Trinh Street (GPS: 21.0243° N, 105.8532° E).

2. Vegan Cooking Class: 23 Bat Su Street (GPS: 21.0359° N, 105.8468° E).

3. Bloom Vegan Hanoi: 33 Hang Buom Street (GPS: 21.0366° N, 105.8516° E).

- Dining Tips: Ask about substitutions for specific ingredients if you have dietary restrictions.

5. Hanoi Coffee and Dessert Tour

- Highlights: A fun exploration of Hanoi's coffee culture, featuring Egg Coffee and sweet treats like Che (Vietnamese dessert soup).
- Price Range: $20 - $30 per tour.
- Where to Book:

1. Hanoi Coffee Tours: 64 Luong Van Can Street (GPS: 21.0312° N, 105.8501° E).

2. Café Giang Tour: 39 Nguyen Huu Huan Street (GPS: 21.0334° N, 105.8510° E).

3. Hanoi Dessert Walk: 21 Hang Gai Street (GPS: 21.0337° N, 105.8519° E).

Dining Etiquette: Coffee culture is casual; linger over your cup and enjoy the conversation.

Useful Phrases for Visitors
- "Tôi muốn học nấu món này." (I want to learn to cook this dish.)
- "Bao nhiêu tiền?" (How much does it cost?)
- "Cảm ơn!" (Thank you!)

These food tours and classes offer an authentic way to experience Hanoi's rich culinary heritage while gaining new skills to take home.

CHAPTER 5

Shopping and Souvenirs

Hanoi is a shopper's haven, offering bustling markets, exquisite handcrafted goods, and vibrant boutiques. From Dong Xuan Market to hidden workshops, the city brims with opportunities to find unique souvenirs. This chapter guides you through Hanoi's shopping scene, from selecting authentic treasures to mastering the art of bargaining like a local.

Hanoi's Best Markets: Dong Xuan and Night Markets

Hanoi's markets are vibrant hubs for shopping and cultural experiences, offering everything from local crafts to street food. Here's a guide to five of the city's best markets.

1. Dong Xuan Market
Description: This multi-level indoor market is Hanoi's largest, perfect for wholesale goods, souvenirs, and local food stalls.

- Location: 15B Dong Xuan Street, Hoan Kiem District (GPS: 21.0380° N, 105.8476° E).
- Contact: +84 24 3825 3517.
- How to Get There: A 10-minute walk from Hoan Kiem Lake or take a taxi.
- What to Shop For: Textiles, traditional hats, and handicrafts.
- Opening Hours: Daily, 6:00 AM - 6:00 PM.
- Payment Methods: Cash preferred; some vendors accept local e-wallets.
- Tips: Start bargaining at 50% of the asking price.

2. Hanoi Weekend Night Market
- Description: Spanning several streets, this bustling night market is known for street food, clothing, and souvenirs.
- Location: Hang Dao Street to Dong Xuan Market (GPS: 21.0347° N, 105.8475° E).
- How to Get There: Walk from the Old Quarter or take a cyclo for an authentic experience.
- What to Shop For: Jewelry, hand-painted items, and Vietnamese snacks.
- Opening Hours: Friday to Sunday, 6:00 PM - 11:00 PM.
- Payment Methods: Cash only.

- Tips: Go early to avoid crowds and explore street food vendors.

3. Quang Ba Flower Market
- Description: A fragrant, colorful market selling fresh flowers from across Vietnam.
- Location: Au Co Street, Tay Ho District (GPS: 21.0631° N, 105.8458° E).
- Contact: +84 24 3719 3047.
- How to Get There: A 20-minute taxi ride from the city center.
- What to Shop For: Fresh flowers, plants, and floral arrangements.
- Opening Hours: Daily, 2:00 AM - 6:00 AM.
- Payment Methods: Cash only.
- Tips: Best visited before sunrise for the freshest blooms.

4. Cho Hom Market
- Description: A textile haven for fabrics, traditional ao dai materials, and clothing accessories.
- Location: Hue Street, Hai Ba Trung District (GPS: 21.0145° N, 105.8504° E).
- How to Get There: Take a bus or taxi from Hoan Kiem Lake.

- What to Shop For: Tailoring fabrics and household items.
- Opening Hours: Daily, 6:00 AM - 6:00 PM.
- Payment Methods: Cash preferred; limited card acceptance.
- Tips: Bring a calculator for accurate price negotiation.

5. Long Bien Market
- Description: A bustling wholesale market offering fresh produce, seafood, and snacks.
- Location: Long Bien Bridge area, Hoan Kiem District (GPS: 21.0416° N, 105.8509° E).
- How to Get There: A short taxi ride from the Old Quarter.
- What to Shop For: Fresh fruits, vegetables, and dry goods.
- Opening Hours: Daily, 1:00 AM - 6:00 AM.
- Payment Methods: Cash only.
- Tips: Ideal for early risers who want to experience local trading culture.

General Tips for Hanoi Markets
- Currency Exchange: Exchange money at banks or authorized forex counters beforehand; US dollars are rarely accepted.
- Safety: Keep belongings secure and be aware of pickpockets in crowded areas.
- Haggling Etiquette: Greet vendors with "Xin chào" (Hello) and say "Bao nhiêu tiền?" (How much does it cost?). Politely negotiate by smiling and maintaining a friendly tone.

2. Authentic Souvenirs: Silk, Art, and Handicrafts

Hanoi is an ideal city to shop for authentic souvenirs that reflect Vietnam's artistry and culture. From luxurious silk to intricate handicrafts, here are the top five souvenirs and where to find them.

1. Silk Products

Description: Hanoi silk is known for its softness, vibrant colors, and durability. You can buy scarves, ties, or tailor-made ao dai.

Where to Get It:

1. Van Phuc Silk Village: Van Phuc, Ha Dong District (GPS: 20.9680° N, 105.7697° E).

2. Hang Gai Street: Old Quarter, Hoan Kiem District (GPS: 21.0341° N, 105.8495° E).

- How to Get There: Take a taxi or bus from the city center to Van Phuc, or walk to Hang Gai Street if staying near Hoan Kiem Lake.
- Other Things to Shop For: Custom-tailored clothing and fabric rolls.
- Opening Hours: Daily, 8:00 AM - 6:00 PM.
- Payment Methods: Cash and cards are widely accepted.

2. Vietnamese Paintings

Description: Local art often depicts rural landscapes, historical scenes, or modern interpretations of Vietnamese culture.

Where to Get It:

1. Art Vietnam Gallery: 2 Hang Bong Street (GPS: 21.0315° N, 105.8471° E).

2. Dong Xuan Market: 15B Dong Xuan Street (GPS: 21.0380° N, 105.8476° E).

- How to Get There: Use taxis or motorbike taxis for direct access.
- Other Things to Shop For: Lacquerware and calligraphy art.
- Opening Hours: Galleries open 9:00 AM - 7:00 PM; markets close at 6:00 PM.
- Payment Methods: Cash and major credit cards.

3. Hand-Embroidery

Description: Hand-embroidered tablecloths, pillowcases, and wall hangings showcase meticulous craftsmanship.

Where to Get It:

1. Tan My Design: 61 Hang Gai Street (GPS: 21.0342° N, 105.8494° E).

2. Craft Link: 43 Van Mieu Street (GPS: 21.0287° N, 105.8413° E).

- How to Get There: A short walk from Hoan Kiem Lake or a taxi ride to Van Mieu Street.
- Other Things to Shop For: Handmade bags and accessories.
- Opening Hours: Daily, 9:00 AM - 8:00 PM.
- Payment Methods: Cards accepted in most shops.

4. Bamboo and Rattan Products

- Description: Eco-friendly baskets, trays, and furniture crafted from natural bamboo and rattan.
- Where to Get It:

1. Bat Trang Ceramic Village: Gia Lam District (GPS: 20.9937° N, 105.9382° E).

2. Dong Xuan Market: 15B Dong Xuan Street (GPS: 21.0380° N, 105.8476° E).

- How to Get There: A 30-minute taxi ride to Bat Trang or a short walk to Dong Xuan Market.
- Other Things to Shop For: Ceramic ware.
- Opening Hours: Daily, 8:00 AM - 5:00 PM.
- Payment Methods: Mostly cash.

5. Vietnamese Coffee

- Description: Famous for its bold flavor, you can buy ground coffee or whole beans from local plantations.
- Where to Get It:

1. Huong Mai Coffee: 15 Hang Manh Street (GPS: 21.0352° N, 105.8477° E).

2. Trung Nguyen Coffee House: Various locations (GPS varies).

- How to Get There: Easily accessible via a walk or short taxi ride.

- Other Things to Shop For: Traditional coffee filters.
- Opening Hours: 8:00 AM - 9:00 PM.
- Payment Methods: Cards and cash.

Shopping Tips

- Safety: Keep an eye on your belongings in crowded areas.
- Haggling Etiquette: Start with half the price offered and negotiate politely.
- Useful Phrases:
- "Cái này bao nhiêu?" (How much is this?)
- "Có giảm giá không?" (Can you give me a discount?)

3. Exploring Boutiques and Local Designers

Hanoi's boutique scene reflects a creative blend of tradition and modernity. Local designers and small shops offer handcrafted fashion, home decor, and unique souvenirs that stand out. Here are five boutiques and designers worth visiting.

1. Chula Fashion
- Description: Chula is known for its bold, colorful designs inspired by Vietnamese culture, combining silk and other high-quality fabrics.
- Where to Find It:

Address: 43 Nhat Chieu Street, Tay Ho District (GPS: 21.0531° N, 105.8227° E).

- How to Get There: A 20-minute taxi ride from the Old Quarter.
- Other Things to Shop For: Jewelry and accessories complementing their outfits.
- Opening Hours: Daily, 9:00 AM - 7:00 PM.
- Payment Methods: Cash, cards, and e-wallets.

2. Kilomet109
- Description: This boutique offers sustainable fashion using natural dyes and handwoven textiles crafted by Vietnamese artisans.
- Where to Find It:

Address: 27 To Ngoc Van Street, Tay Ho District (GPS: 21.0598° N, 105.8270° E).

- How to Get There: A short taxi ride from Hoan Kiem Lake.

- Other Things to Shop For: Hand-dyed scarves and organic cotton pieces.
- Opening Hours: Daily, 10:00 AM - 8:00 PM.
- Payment Methods: Cards and cash.

3. Module 7
- Description: A boutique for contemporary home decor and fashion, blending modern design with traditional Vietnamese craftsmanship.
- Where to Find It:

Address: 83 Xuan Dieu Street, Tay Ho District (GPS: 21.0580° N, 105.8256° E).
- How to Get There: A 15-minute taxi ride from the Old Quarter.
- Other Things to Shop For: Decorative ceramics and minimalist furniture.
- Opening Hours: Daily, 9:00 AM - 6:00 PM.
- Payment Methods: Cash and major credit cards.

4. Hanoi Design Centre

Description: A showcase of contemporary Vietnamese design, featuring products from independent local designers.

Where to Find It:

Address: 2 Hang Bong Street, Hoan Kiem District (GPS: 21.0315° N, 105.8470° E).

- How to Get There: Easily walkable from Hoan Kiem Lake.
- Other Things to Shop For: Art prints and handmade jewelry.
- Opening Hours: Daily, 9:30 AM - 7:30 PM.
- Payment Methods: Cards, cash, and e-wallets.

5. Tan My Design

- Description: A family-run boutique offering hand-embroidered clothing, home goods, and gifts.
- Where to Find It:

Address: 61 Hang Gai Street, Hoan Kiem District (GPS: 21.0342° N, 105.8494° E).

- How to Get There: Walkable from the Old Quarter.
- Other Things to Shop For: Linen tablecloths and embroidered accessories.
- Opening Hours: Daily, 9:00 AM - 8:00 PM.
- Payment Methods: Cash and cards.

Shopping Tips
- Bargaining: Bargaining is less common in boutiques, but asking for small discounts on multiple purchases is acceptable.
- Safety: Keep personal items secure in busy shopping areas.
- Useful Phrases:
- "Cái này bao nhiêu?" (How much is this?)
- "Có giảm giá không?" (Can you give a discount?)

4. Tips for Bargaining Like a Local

Shopping in Hanoi's bustling markets and shops often includes bargaining, a common practice that's almost an art form. Here's how to negotiate confidently while respecting local customs and ensuring a good deal.

1. Start with a Friendly Greeting

Why It Matters: A polite introduction can set the tone for a friendly exchange. Greet the vendor with "Xin chào" (Hello) and smile. Building rapport often leads to a smoother negotiation process.

2. Know the Value of the Item
- Where to Research: Visit larger markets like Dong Xuan Market (15B Dong Xuan Street, GPS: 21.0380° N, 105.8476° E) to get an idea of general prices before you start bargaining.
- How to Get There: A short walk or taxi ride from Hoan Kiem Lake.
- Opening Hours: Daily, 6:00 AM - 6:00 PM.
- What Else to Shop For: Clothing, souvenirs, and home goods.

3. Offer Half, Then Work Your Way Up

How to Approach: Begin by offering 50-60% of the initial price, then gradually increase your offer. Vendors often quote higher prices expecting a negotiation.

4. Stay Calm and Polite
- What to Avoid: Avoid being aggressive or overly insistent. If the price doesn't meet your expectations, thank the vendor and walk away. Often, they'll call you back with a better offer.
- Where This Works Best: Hanoi Weekend Night Market (Hang Dao Street to Dong Xuan Market, GPS: 21.0347° N, 105.8475° E).

- Opening Hours: Friday to Sunday, 6:00 PM - 11:00 PM.
- What Else to Shop For: Jewelry, handmade items, and snacks.

5. Bring Cash and Small Denominations
- Why It Helps: Vendors often prefer cash, and having smaller bills makes negotiations smoother. Ensure you exchange currency at a reliable forex counter or bank beforehand.
- Safety Tip: Keep your money in a secure place to avoid pickpockets in busy markets.

Useful Phrases
- "Bao nhiêu tiền?" (How much is this?)
- "Có giảm giá không?" (Can you give me a discount?)
- "Tôi không muốn mua." (I don't want to buy it.)

Final Thoughts

Bargaining is a part of the shopping experience in Hanoi, but always keep it lighthearted and respectful. By approaching it with a friendly attitude and understanding local customs, you'll leave with not only great deals but also enjoyable interactions with Hanoi's lively vendors.

CHAPTER 6

Beyond the City – Hanoi's Day Trips

Hanoi offers more than its vibrant streets—its surroundings are filled with fascinating destinations. From the serene waters of Ha Long Bay to the lush landscapes of Ninh Binh, the spiritual Perfume Pagoda, and the craftsmanship of Bat Trang Ceramic Village, these day trips promise memorable experiences just a short journey away.

Ha Long Bay: Majestic Waters and Limestone Cliffs

Ha Long Bay, a UNESCO World Heritage Site, is famous for its emerald waters and dramatic limestone karsts. Located just 170 kilometers from Hanoi, it offers an unparalleled escape into nature with opportunities for kayaking, hiking, and exploring caves.

Best Places for Outdoor Adventures
- Titov Island: Known for its panoramic views after a short hike to the top.

- Sung Sot (Surprise) Cave: A massive grotto with impressive rock formations.
- Luon Cave: Perfect for kayaking through its tranquil waters.

Brief Overview and Costs

- Activities: Kayaking, overnight cruises, swimming, and cave tours.
- Costs:
- Day trip: $40–$60 per person.
- Overnight cruises: $100–$300 depending on luxury level.

Seasonal Considerations

- Best Time to Visit: October to April for cooler, dry weather.
- Avoid: June to August due to potential storms.

Safety Tips and Guidelines

- Wear life jackets during boating or kayaking activities.
- Check weather forecasts before booking trips, as cancellations can occur during storms.
- Stick with experienced guides for cave exploration and hiking.

Permits and Regulations

Permits are usually included in guided tours and cruises. Independent travelers should verify fees with the Halong Bay Management Board.

Difficulty Level

Most activities are beginner-friendly, though hikes on Titov Island may require moderate fitness.

Expected Duration

Day trips last 10–12 hours (including transit from Hanoi). Overnight cruises offer 1- or 2-night stays.

Packing List

- Comfortable walking shoes for hikes.
- Swimwear, sunscreen, and a hat for outdoor activities.
- Light rain gear and insect repellent.
- Reusable water bottles to minimize waste.

Environmental Awareness

Help protect the bay by avoiding single-use plastics and respecting "leave no trace" principles. Dispose of waste responsibly to preserve this natural treasure.

Emergency Contacts
- Ha Long Bay Tourism Office: +84 33 845 845.
- Coast Guard Hotline: 112.

Recommended Tour Operators

1. Indochina Junk (http://www.indochina-junk.com)
   Contact: +84 24 3933 6260.
2. Bhaya Cruises
   Website: http://www.bhayacruises.com)
   Contact: +84 24 3944 6777.
3. Halong Bay Cruise Hunters
   Website: http://www.halongbaycruisehunters.com)
   Contact: +84 96 773 8225.

2. Ninh Binh: Pagodas, Rice Fields, and Boat Rides

Ninh Binh, just 100 kilometers south of Hanoi, is often called the "Inland Ha Long Bay" for its breathtaking karst formations, lush rice fields, and historic temples. A favorite for nature lovers and history buffs, this area promises a tranquil escape from the city.

Best Places for Outdoor Adventures

- Trang An Scenic Landscape Complex: Enjoy a serene boat ride through caves and limestone peaks.
- Tam Coc: Known as "three caves," this area offers stunning views of rice paddies from a boat.
- Bai Dinh Pagoda: One of the largest Buddhist complexes in Southeast Asia, with intricate architecture and panoramic views.

Brief Overview and Costs

- Activities: Rowing boat rides, temple visits, and cycling tours.
- Costs:
- Boat ride: $8–$12 per person.
- Entrance to Bai Dinh: $5. Electric car transfers available for an additional $2.

Seasonal Considerations

- Best Time to Visit: May and June for vibrant green rice fields or September for golden harvest views.
- Avoid: Rainy season (July-August) due to slippery paths and potential flooding.

Safety Tips and Guidelines

- Wear life jackets during boat rides.
- Keep hydrated and apply sunscreen, especially during hotter months.
- Follow posted signs and stay within designated areas at temples and caves.

Permits and Regulations

Most attractions include permit fees in the ticket price. For independent cycling or hiking, check with local guides for any additional requirements.

Difficulty Level

- Boat rides and temple visits are suitable for all ages.
- Cycling routes may require moderate fitness due to uneven terrain.

Expected Duration

- Day trips from Hanoi last 10–12 hours.
- Overnight stays are recommended for a more relaxed itinerary.

Packing List

- Comfortable walking shoes and lightweight clothing.
- A hat, sunscreen, and insect repellent for outdoor activities.
- Reusable water bottles to minimize waste.

Environmental Awareness

Respect the natural surroundings by not littering. Avoid touching or disturbing wildlife during tours.

Emergency Contacts

- Ninh Binh Tourist Information: +84 229 387 4499.
- Local Police Hotline: 113.

Recommended Tour Operators

1. Ninh Binh Getaway

   Website: http://www.ninhbinhgetaway.com)

   Contact: +84 96 955 5225.

2. Trang An Boat Tours

   Website: http://www.tranganboat.com)

   Contact: +84 229 361 2222.

3. Bai Dinh Cycling Tours

   Website: http://www.baidinhcycling.com)

   Contact: +84 98 881 7722.

Ninh Binh combines natural beauty with cultural depth, making it a perfect getaway to unwind and explore Vietnam's rich heritage.

3. Perfume Pagoda: A Scenic Pilgrimage

The Perfume Pagoda, or Chùa Hương, is a spiritual retreat just 60 kilometers southwest of Hanoi. Set amidst dramatic limestone mountains and lush greenery, it's both a pilgrimage site and a natural haven, offering visitors a mix of cultural exploration and outdoor adventure.

Best Places for Outdoor Adventures
- Huong Tich Cave: The main shrine, located deep inside a limestone grotto, revered for its spiritual significance and breathtaking beauty.
- Yen Stream: A tranquil boat ride through peaceful waterways flanked by lush hills.
- Thien Tru Pagoda: A picturesque temple on the way to the main site.

Brief Overview and Costs
- Activities: Rowing boat rides, trekking, and visiting pagodas.
- Costs:
- Entrance fee: $3 per person.
- Boat ride: $3–$5 per person (round trip).
- Cable car (optional): $4 one way, $6 round trip.

Seasonal Considerations

- Best Time to Visit: February to April during the Perfume Pagoda Festival when the atmosphere is lively with pilgrims.
- Avoid: Rainy season (July–August) as trails can become slippery.

Safety Tips and Guidelines

- Wear sturdy shoes for hiking, as the trek to Huong Tich Cave involves uneven steps.
- Follow guides and official signs to avoid straying from safe paths.
- Stay hydrated, especially during the warmer months.

Permits and Regulations

Entrance fees are mandatory and collected at the site. Additional permits are not required for most visitors.

Difficulty Level

The trek to Huong Tich Cave is moderately challenging, with an option to use a cable car for easier access.

Expected Duration

- Day trips from Hanoi last about 8–10 hours.
- Allocate 3–4 hours at the site itself, including travel time by boat and on foot.

Packing List

- Comfortable walking shoes and lightweight clothing.
- Rain gear and insect repellent if visiting during the wet season.
- Snacks and water, as food options may be limited.

Environmental Awareness

Avoid littering and use designated trash bins. Respect the sanctity of the site by keeping noise levels low and adhering to local customs.

Emergency Contacts

- Local Tourism Office: +84 24 3851 1223.
- Police Hotline: 113.

Recommended Tour Operators

1. Hanoi Eco Tours

   Website: (http://www.hanoiecotours.com)

   Contact: +84 96 886 5523.

2. Vietnam Nomad Trails

   Website: http://www.vietnamnomadtrails.com)

   Contact: +84 98 889 1122.

3. Asia Outdoors

   Website: http://www.asiaoutdoors.com)

   Contact: +84 93 666 7725.

The Perfume Pagoda offers a peaceful escape, blending cultural richness with natural splendor, making it an unforgettable part of any Hanoi visit.

4. Bat Trang Ceramic Village: Traditional Craftsmanship

Located just 13 kilometers southeast of Hanoi, Bat Trang Ceramic Village is a renowned hub for ceramic art, boasting over 700 years of history. This quaint village offers an immersive experience into Vietnam's pottery traditions, perfect for visitors looking to learn about the craft and take home unique handmade items.

Best Places for Outdoor Adventures
- Pottery Workshops: Try your hand at shaping clay or painting ceramic pieces.
- Bat Trang Market: Explore stalls showcasing plates, bowls, vases, and art pieces.

- Ceramic Museum: A modern building featuring intricate designs and historical displays.

Brief Overview and Costs
- Activities: Hands-on pottery-making, shopping, and museum visits.
- Costs:
- Pottery workshop: $2–$5 per session.
- Museum entrance: Free or minimal fees depending on exhibits.
- Handmade ceramics: Prices vary from $1 to $50, depending on the item.

Seasonal Considerations
- Best Time to Visit: October to March for cooler weather and a comfortable shopping experience.
- Avoid: Rainy months (July–August), as outdoor areas can be muddy.

Safety Tips and Guidelines
- Handle ceramics with care to avoid accidental breakages.
- Wear comfortable shoes, as some paths can be uneven.
- Keep an eye on small children during workshops.

Permits and Regulations

Entry to the village is free, and workshops or museum visits typically include all necessary fees.

Difficulty Level

Activities like pottery-making are beginner-friendly, suitable for all ages.

Expected Duration

A half-day trip (4–6 hours) is sufficient to explore workshops, markets, and museums.

Packing List

- A reusable bag for carrying purchased ceramics.
- Comfortable walking shoes.
- Weather-appropriate clothing (rain gear during wet months).

Environmental Awareness

Support sustainable practices by purchasing items from local artisans and avoiding mass-produced goods. Use reusable bags to minimize plastic waste.

Emergency Contacts

- Local Tourism Hotline: +84 24 3936 6888.
- Local Police: 113.

Recommended Tour Operators

1. Hanoi Ceramic Tours
   Website: http://www.hanoiceramictours.com)
   Contact: +84 97 889 5523.
2. Bat Trang Experience
   Website: http://www.battrangexperience.com)
   Contact: +84 96 661 7721.
3. Vietnam Handicraft Tours
   Website: http://www.vietnamhandicrafttours.com)
   Contact: +84 93 777 1124.

Bat Trang Ceramic Village offers a rich blend of creativity, history, and hands-on experiences, making it an ideal stop for cultural enthusiasts and shoppers alike.

CHAPTER 7

Nature and Relaxation in Hanoi

Hanoi offers a balance of vibrant energy and peaceful retreats. Whether strolling by the tranquil waters of Hoan Kiem or West Lake, exploring hidden gardens, sipping coffee with panoramic views, or unwinding in luxurious spas, this chapter highlights the city's best spots for relaxation and reconnecting with nature.

1. Hoan Kiem Lake and West Lake: Scenic Escapes

Hanoi's lakes are serene sanctuaries amidst the city's buzz. Hoan Kiem Lake offers a tranquil spot for reflection and cultural discovery, while West Lake provides expansive views and opportunities for outdoor fun. Together, they highlight Hanoi's harmony between nature and urban life.

Best Places for Outdoor Adventures
- Hoan Kiem Lake: Known for its peaceful pathways, the iconic Turtle Tower, and the historic Ngoc Son Temple, accessible by the red Huc Bridge.

- West Lake (Ho Tay): Hanoi's largest lake, ideal for cycling, jogging, or enjoying waterside cafés.

Brief Overview and Costs

- Activities: Strolling, cycling, photography, and temple visits.
- Costs:

Ngoc Son Temple entrance fee: $1.

West Lake activities, such as bike rentals, range from $3–$5 per hour.

Seasonal Considerations

- Best Time to Visit: October to April for cooler weather and clear skies.
- Avoid: Midday heat in summer (June–August) unless seeking shade in nearby cafés.

Safety Tips and Guidelines

- Keep an eye on belongings, especially in crowded areas near Hoan Kiem Lake.
- Stick to designated pathways and avoid venturing into areas marked restricted.
- If cycling around West Lake, be cautious of traffic near main roads.

Permits and Regulations

Entry to both lakes is free, with Ngoc Son Temple requiring a small ticket fee.

Difficulty Level

Activities like walking and cycling are easy, suitable for all fitness levels.

Expected Duration

- Hoan Kiem Lake: 1–2 hours, including a temple visit.
- West Lake: 2–4 hours, depending on chosen activities.

Packing List

- Comfortable walking shoes.
- Sunscreen, a hat, and sunglasses for sunny days.
- A water bottle to stay hydrated.

Environmental Awareness

Respect the environment by avoiding littering and using designated bins. Support local vendors by purchasing responsibly.

Emergency Contacts

- Tourist Information Hotline: +84 24 3936 6888.
- Local Police: 113.

Recommended Tour Operators

1. Hanoi Walks and Tours
   Website: http://www.hanoiwalksandtours.com)
   Contact: +84 97 885 6622.
2. Vietnam Outdoor Adventures
   Website: http://www.vietnamoutdoor.com)
   Contact: +84 96 668 7723.
3. Eco Hanoi Cycling Tours
   Website: http://www.ecohanoitours.com)
   Contact: +84 93 999 1124.

Whether you're enjoying a quiet moment by Hoan Kiem or biking around West Lake, these scenic spots offer a refreshing escape from Hanoi's bustling streets.

2. Hanoi's Green Spaces: Parks, Gardens, and Hidden Retreats

Amid Hanoi's bustling streets, its green spaces provide peaceful retreats for relaxation, outdoor activities, and fresh air. From historic parks to quiet gardens, these spaces reflect the city's balance of culture and nature.

Best Places for Outdoor Adventures

- Lenin Park (Thong Nhat Park): A large public park with a lake and walking paths, perfect for jogging, picnics, or renting paddle boats.
- Botanical Garden (Vuon Bach Thao): Known for its lush greenery, peaceful trails, and a small lake ideal for unwinding.
- Huu Tiep Lake and B52 Wreck: A hidden gem surrounded by greenery, offering a glimpse of history with a sunken B52 plane.

Brief Overview and Costs

- Activities: Walking, cycling, picnicking, and enjoying natural surroundings.
- Costs:

Lenin Park entrance: Free or $0.50 for specific activities.

Botanical Garden: $1 per person.

Huu Tiep Lake: Free.

Seasonal Considerations

- Best Time to Visit: Early mornings or late afternoons for cooler weather and fewer crowds, especially from October to March.
- Avoid: Midday during summer (June–August), as temperatures can be high.

Safety Tips and Guidelines
- Wear comfortable shoes for walking.
- Keep belongings secure in popular areas to avoid petty theft.
- Carry insect repellent, especially during the rainy season.

Permits and Regulations

No special permits are required, and entry fees are minimal. For larger parks like Lenin Park, specific activities (e.g., paddle boating) may have small additional fees.

Difficulty Level

Activities are generally easy and suitable for all ages.

Expected Duration
- Spend 1–2 hours in each location, depending on your interests and pace.

Packing List
- Lightweight clothing, a hat, and sunglasses.
- A reusable water bottle.
- Snacks for picnics if desired.

Environmental Awareness

Help maintain these spaces by not littering and using designated trash bins. Respect the tranquility of gardens by avoiding loud noises.

Emergency Contacts

- Tourist Hotline: +84 24 3936 6888.
- Local Police: 113.

Recommended Tour Operators

1. Hanoi Walking Tours

   Website: (http://www.hanoi-walkingtours.com)

   Contact: +84 97 885 8822.

2. Eco-Friendly Vietnam

   Website: http://www.ecofriendlyvietnam.com)

   Contact: +84 96 667 7721.

Hanoi's parks and gardens are perfect for slowing down, enjoying nature, and experiencing a quieter side of the city. They offer refreshing breaks that complement the city's lively energy.

3. Rooftop Bars and Cafés: Unwind with a View

Hanoi's skyline transforms into a spectacle when viewed from above, making rooftop bars and cafés the perfect spots to relax. Whether sipping a cocktail or enjoying Vietnamese coffee, these elevated spaces offer breathtaking views of the city's landmarks.

Best Places for Outdoor Adventures
- The Summit Bar: Located at Pan Pacific Hanoi, this bar offers panoramic views of West Lake and the Red River.
- Skyline Hanoi: Overlooking Hoan Kiem Lake, this rooftop spot combines vibrant energy with iconic views.
- Cafe Pho Co: A hidden gem with a quaint rooftop that overlooks Hoan Kiem Lake and the city streets below.

Brief Overview and Costs
- Activities: Enjoying drinks, light meals, and soaking in the scenery.
- Costs:

Cocktails: $5–$12.

Coffee or tea: $2–$5.

Small bites: $3–$8.

Seasonal Considerations
- Best Time to Visit: Early evenings for sunset views, especially between October and April when the skies are clearer.
- Avoid: Rainy days, as outdoor seating may be unavailable.

Safety Tips and Guidelines
- Always confirm seating arrangements during peak hours to secure a good spot.
- Be cautious on staircases or rooftop edges, particularly with children.
- Keep valuables close, as some rooftops can become crowded.

Permits and Regulations

No special permits are required. Some high-end bars may have dress codes, so check in advance.

Difficulty Level

Activities are effortless and accessible for all visitors.

Expected Duration

Spend 1–2 hours enjoying the views and atmosphere.

Packing List
- A light jacket for cooler evenings.
- A camera or smartphone for photos.
- Sunglasses for daytime visits.

Environmental Awareness

Support local establishments by choosing small, locally-owned cafés. Avoid using single-use plastics by bringing a reusable straw or cup if needed.

Emergency Contacts

- Tourism Hotline: +84 24 3936 6888.
- Local Police: 113.

Recommended Tour Operators

1. Hanoi Rooftop Experiences

   Website: http://www.hanoirooftopexperiences.com)

   Contact: +84 97 889 5523.

2. Skyline Views Hanoi

   Website: http://www.skylineviewshanoi.com)

   Contact: +84 96 668 7721.

Unwinding at a rooftop bar or café is a great way to see Hanoi from a fresh perspective. Whether enjoying the vibrant city lights or the peaceful sunset, it's a memorable addition to your trip.

4. Wellness and Spa Experiences in the City

Hanoi offers a serene side for those seeking relaxation and rejuvenation. With a blend of traditional Vietnamese therapies and modern wellness techniques, the city's spas and wellness centers provide a peaceful escape from the bustling streets.

Best Places for Outdoor Adventures
- Sen Garden Spa: Located near West Lake, this spa offers garden-themed treatments for a tranquil atmosphere.
- La Spa Hanoi: Known for its traditional Vietnamese massages and organic products.
- Anam QT Spa: A luxurious retreat in the Old Quarter offering a wide range of therapeutic options.

Brief Overview and Costs
- Activities: Massages, facials, herbal baths, and yoga sessions.
- Costs:

Traditional Vietnamese massage: $15–$30.

Full spa packages: $50–$100.

Seasonal Considerations

- Best Time to Visit: Year-round, but a spa day is especially refreshing after outdoor adventures in Hanoi's summer heat or during the cooler months for relaxation.
- Avoid: Peak evening hours if you prefer a quieter experience.

Safety Tips and Guidelines

- Confirm the spa's hygiene standards and ensure therapists are certified.
- Inform therapists of any medical conditions or allergies before starting treatments.
- Keep valuables secure, as some wellness centers may not provide lockers.

Permits and Regulations

No permits are required, but high-end spas may require reservations, especially during weekends or holidays.

Difficulty Level

All activities are suitable for any age or fitness level, focusing on comfort and relaxation.

Expected Duration

Most treatments last 1–2 hours, while full-day spa experiences can take up to 5 hours.

Packing List

- Comfortable, loose clothing for post-treatment relaxation.
- A reusable water bottle to stay hydrated.

Environmental Awareness

Support spas that use eco-friendly products and avoid single-use plastics. Many wellness centers in Hanoi focus on sustainable practices—ask about their initiatives.

Emergency Contacts

- Hanoi Tourism Hotline: +84 24 3936 6888.
- Local Police: 113.

Recommended Tour Operators

1. Hanoi Wellness Retreats

   Website: http://www.hanoiwellnessretreats.com)

   Contact: +84 97 888 6612.

2. Vietnam Spa Trails

   Website: http://www.vietnamspatrails.com)

   Contact: +84 96 887 5523.

Taking time to relax in one of Hanoi's wellness centers is a gift to yourself. From herbal baths to traditional massages, these experiences will leave you refreshed and ready for more adventures.

CHAPTER 8

Adventure and Activities in Hanoi

Hanoi offers exciting activities for every traveler, from motorbike tours that zip through bustling streets to serene walking trails and hidden rooftop views. Explore the city's lesser-known corners, vibrant urban life, and colorful seasonal festivals that bring its culture to life, creating unforgettable adventures at every turn.

1. Motorbike Tours: Thrills on Two Wheels

Motorbike tours are one of the most exhilarating ways to experience Hanoi. These guided adventures let you weave through the city's vibrant streets, sample authentic street food, and explore cultural landmarks, offering a dynamic view of the city from the back of a motorbike.

Best Places for Outdoor Adventures
- Old Quarter: Navigate the lively streets filled with historic architecture and buzzing markets.
- West Lake: A scenic ride along the lake's edge, perfect for photos and a refreshing breeze.

- Long Bien Bridge: Cross this iconic steel structure, offering views of the Red River and local life along its banks.

Brief Overview and Costs

- Activities: City tours, food-focused rides, or countryside day trips.
- Costs:

Half-day city tour: $35–$50 per person.

Full-day countryside tour: $60–$100, including meals.

Seasonal Considerations

- Best Time to Ride: October to April for mild weather and less humidity.
- Avoid: Rainy days (July–August), as wet roads can make riding slippery.

Safety Tips and Guidelines

- Always wear a helmet provided by your tour operator.
- Follow your guide's instructions and avoid risky maneuvers in heavy traffic.
- Wear closed-toe shoes and comfortable clothing to protect yourself during the ride.

Permits and Regulations

No special permits are needed for passengers. Drivers must have a valid international driving permit if planning to self-ride.

Difficulty Level

The tours are beginner-friendly, as you'll ride with experienced drivers. Self-riding tours may require intermediate skills due to Hanoi's traffic.

Expected Duration

- Half-day tours last 3–4 hours.
- Full-day tours cover 6–8 hours with breaks for meals and sightseeing.

Packing List

- Sunglasses to shield your eyes from dust.
- A light jacket for cooler evenings.
- A reusable water bottle.

Environmental Awareness

Support sustainable tours that minimize environmental impact, such as operators using electric bikes or focusing on local, eco-friendly experiences.

Emergency Contacts

- Tourist Information Hotline: +84 24 3936 6888.
- Local Police: 113.

Recommended Tour Operators

1. Hanoi Motorbike Tours

   Website: http://www.hanoimotorbiketours.com)

   Contact: +84 97 885 6622.

2. Motorbike Hanoi Adventures

   Website: http://www.motorbikehanoi.com)

   Contact: +84 96 661 7721.

3. Vietnam Easy Riders

   Website: http://www.vietnameasyriders.com)

   Contact: +84 93 777 1124.

Exploring Hanoi on two wheels offers a rush of freedom while connecting you to the city's vibrant energy. It's a thrilling way to see Hanoi beyond the usual paths.

2. Walking Trails and Urban Exploration

Exploring Hanoi on foot is one of the most rewarding ways to experience its history, culture, and daily life. From the bustling streets of the Old Quarter to peaceful lakeside paths,

Hanoi's walking trails offer a mix of urban charm and tranquil escapes.

Best Places for Outdoor Adventures
- Old Quarter: Wander through narrow streets filled with colonial-era buildings, traditional shops, and lively markets.
- Hoan Kiem Lake: A leisurely walk around the lake is perfect for a quiet morning or evening stroll.
- Ba Dinh District: Visit iconic landmarks like the Ho Chi Minh Mausoleum, Presidential Palace, and One Pillar Pagoda.

Brief Overview and Costs
- Activities: Walking tours, photography, cultural exploration, and food stops.
- Costs:
- Self-guided walks: Free.
- Guided tours: $15–$30 per person, depending on duration and itinerary.

Seasonal Considerations
- Best Time to Walk: October to April for cooler weather and less humidity.
- Avoid: Midday in summer (June–August) to avoid heat exhaustion.

Safety Tips and Guidelines
- Stay hydrated and wear sunscreen during daytime walks.
- Use crosswalks and follow traffic signals, as Hanoi's streets can be busy.
- Be cautious with personal belongings in crowded areas to prevent theft.

Permits and Regulations

No permits are required for walking trails. Entry fees apply for certain landmarks, such as the Ho Chi Minh Mausoleum or Ngoc Son Temple ($1–$2).

Difficulty Level

Walking tours are easy to moderate, suitable for most fitness levels. Comfortable shoes are a must.

Expected Duration
- Short walks around Hoan Kiem Lake: 30 minutes to 1 hour.
- Full exploration of the Old Quarter and Ba Dinh District: 2–4 hours.

Packing List
- Comfortable walking shoes.
- Lightweight clothing and a hat.
- A reusable water bottle.

Environmental Awareness

Support sustainable practices by avoiding single-use plastics. Respect the city's heritage by not touching or climbing on historic structures.

Emergency Contacts

- Tourist Information Hotline: +84 24 3936 6888.
- Local Police: 113.

Recommended Tour Operators

1. Hanoi Free Walking Tours
   Website: http://www.hanoifreewalkingtours.com)
   Contact: +84 96 778 8822.
2. Urban Trails Hanoi
   Website: http://www.urbantrailshanoi.com)
   Contact: +84 97 889 5523.

Walking through Hanoi's vibrant streets and serene paths offers a deeper connection to the city's culture and energy. It's an experience that reveals the heart of Hanoi, step by step.

3. Hanoi's Hidden Gems: From Secret Alleys to Rooftop Views

Hanoi is a city of surprises, offering hidden treasures beyond its well-known landmarks. From quiet alleys filled with character to rooftop vistas that showcase the city's beauty, these hidden gems reveal Hanoi's unique blend of tradition and modernity.

Best Places for Outdoor Adventures

1. Train Street
- Brief Overview: A narrow street where daily life thrives around a functioning railway. Visitors can watch trains pass just inches from homes.
- Costs: Free; seating at nearby cafés requires a purchase ($2–$5).
- Seasonal Considerations: Visit between October and April for cooler weather.
- Safety Tips: Stand at a safe distance when trains approach.
- Expected Duration: 1–2 hours.

2. Long Bien Bridge
- Brief Overview: A historic steel bridge with pedestrian pathways offering views of the Red River.
- Costs: Free.
- Seasonal Considerations: Ideal at sunrise or sunset for scenic views.
- Safety Tips: Be cautious of motorbikes on the shared path.
- Expected Duration: 1 hour.

Rooftop Views

Skyline Hanoi
- Brief Overview: A rooftop bar providing panoramic views of the Old Quarter and Hoan Kiem Lake.
- Costs: Drinks range from $5–$12.
- Seasonal Considerations: Sunset hours are the best time for a visit.
- Expected Duration: 1–2 hours.

Practical Information
- Packing List: Comfortable shoes for walking, a reusable water bottle, sunscreen, and a light jacket for evenings.

- Environmental Awareness: Respect local spaces by disposing of waste responsibly and supporting local vendors.

Permits and Regulations

No permits are required for these locations. Train Street visits are managed by local cafés, and rooftop bars have standard entry rules.

Emergency Contacts

- Tourist Hotline: +84 24 3936 6888.
- Local Police: 113.

Recommended Tour Operators

1. Hanoi Hidden Walks

   Website: http://www.hanoihiddenwalks.com)

   Contact: +84 96 789 2211.

2. Skyline Adventures Hanoi

   Website: http://www.skylineadventureshanoi.com)

   Contact: +84 97 788 1153.

These lesser-known spots offer a unique view of Hanoi's charm, blending the energy of its streets with quiet moments and unforgettable perspectives.

4. Seasonal Festivals: Celebrating Hanoi's Vibrant Culture

Hanoi's festivals provide an immersive way to experience its rich traditions, with colorful celebrations and meaningful rituals. From the Lunar New Year to mid-autumn festivities, these events bring the city to life and welcome visitors to join in the vibrant atmosphere.

Key Festivals to Experience

1. Tet Festival (Lunar New Year)
- Introduction: Tet marks the Vietnamese New Year, typically in late January or early February. It's a time for family reunions, honoring ancestors, and welcoming prosperity.
- Date: Dates vary each year based on the lunar calendar.
- Key Venues:
- Hoan Kiem Lake (Address: Hoan Kiem District, GPS: 21.0285° N, 105.8542° E) for fireworks and festive decorations.
- Local pagodas for ceremonial offerings.
- Opening Hours: Most celebrations occur throughout the day and night.

- Dress Code: Wear traditional ao dai or modest, comfortable clothing.
- Etiquette: Bring small gifts like fruit or sweets if invited to a local home. Avoid discussing bad luck or negative topics.

2. Mid-Autumn Festival

- Introduction: A family-oriented event in September celebrating the harvest moon with lantern processions and mooncakes.
- Key Venues:

Hang Ma Street (Address: Hang Ma, Hoan Kiem District, GPS: 21.0354° N, 105.8502° E) for lantern shopping.

Hoan Kiem Lake for parades and performances.

- Opening Hours: Lantern displays are most vibrant after sunset.
- Dress Code: Casual attire with comfortable walking shoes.
- Etiquette: Share mooncakes and enjoy cultural performances.

Practical Tips

Getting Around at Night

Use ride-hailing apps like Grab or local taxis for safe transport. The Old Quarter is walkable for most festival venues.

Budgeting and Expenses

- Fireworks and public displays are free.
- Lanterns or souvenirs cost $2–$10. Mooncakes range from $5–$15.

Local Laws and Regulations

- Avoid littering during festivals, as cleanliness is highly respected.
- Public intoxication is frowned upon, even during celebrations.

Interesting Facts

- Tet celebrations often involve banning scissors or sharp objects as they symbolize cutting ties.
- The Mid-Autumn Festival is believed to bring prosperity and joy for families.

Hanoi's festivals are a blend of joy, culture, and tradition. Joining these events lets you connect with the city's soul while creating unforgettable memories.

CHAPTER 9

The Perfect 5-Day Itinerary

Planning your trip to Hanoi? This 5-day itinerary ensures a balance of cultural experiences, scenic day trips, and leisurely moments. From wandering through the vibrant Old Quarter to enjoying serene lakeside views and savoring street food, each day offers an unforgettable glimpse into the heart of Vietnam's bustling capital.

1. Day 1: Arrival, Exploring the Old Quarter, and a Street Food Tour

Your first day in Hanoi sets the tone for an unforgettable journey. As you arrive, the city's vibrant streets and warm hospitality welcome you. Begin your adventure with a stroll through the Old Quarter, a historical hub buzzing with energy, and indulge in Hanoi's celebrated street food culture.

Arrival in Hanoi

Upon landing at Noi Bai International Airport, you'll find it easy to navigate to the city center. A taxi or Grab ride to the Old Quarter takes about 45 minutes and costs $15–$20.

Shared minivans offer a more economical option at around $5 per person. If you've pre-arranged with your hotel, they may provide a private transfer for added convenience.

Estimated Budget for Arrival: $5–$20.

Exploring the Old Quarter

The Old Quarter is the heart of Hanoi, with its narrow streets, colonial architecture, and vibrant local markets. Spend the afternoon wandering its 36 streets, each traditionally specializing in a specific trade. Highlights include:

- Hang Ma Street: Known for colorful lanterns and traditional decorations.
- Dong Xuan Market: A bustling marketplace perfect for souvenirs and a glimpse of local life.
- St. Joseph's Cathedral: A striking French Gothic structure worth a photo stop.

What to Bring: Comfortable walking shoes, a water bottle, and a camera to capture the lively scenes.

Street Food Tour

As evening falls, dive into Hanoi's legendary street food scene with a guided tour or a self-guided culinary adventure. Local delicacies to try include:

- Pho: Hanoi's iconic noodle soup, available at Pho Thin (13 Lo Duc Street, $2–$3 per bowl).
- Banh Mi: Vietnamese baguette sandwiches stuffed with flavorful fillings, found at Banh Mi 25 (25 Hang Ca Street, $1.50–$2).
- Egg Coffee: A creamy delight at Cafe Giang (39 Nguyen Huu Huan Street, $1.50).

A guided food tour typically costs $20–$25 per person and includes tastings at multiple spots while learning about the dishes' origins and preparation.

Estimated Budget for the Day
- Transport to the city: $5–$20.
- Exploring the Old Quarter: Free (shopping optional).
- Street Food Tour: $10–$25.
- Total: $15–$50, depending on your dining and transport choices.

Tips for the Day
- Dress Comfortably: Hanoi's streets can be busy and warm. Opt for light clothing.
- Stay Safe: Keep your valuables secure while exploring crowded areas.
- Currency Exchange: Ensure you have Vietnamese Dong for small purchases.

Day 1 in Hanoi introduces you to the city's rhythm—its bustling streets, cultural charm, and unforgettable flavors. It's the perfect start to your journey in Vietnam.

2. Day 2: Historical Sites and Lakeside Relaxation

Hanoi is a city where history breathes through its streets and lakes offer moments of peace amidst the urban hustle. Day two of your journey can be devoted to exploring its iconic landmarks and soaking in the calm around its serene lakes.

Morning: Historical Sites
Start your day by visiting some of Hanoi's most famous historical landmarks.

- Ho Chi Minh Mausoleum:

  Pay homage to Vietnam's revolutionary leader at this grand site. Be prepared for long lines and respectful silence inside.

- Location: 2 Hung Vuong Street, Ba Dinh District (GPS: 21.0379° N, 105.8348° E).
- Opening Hours: 7:30 AM – 10:30 AM (closed Mondays and Fridays).
- Entry Fee: Free.
- Tips: Wear modest clothing and arrive early to avoid crowds. Cameras and phones are not allowed inside.

Temple of Literature:

A stunning example of traditional Vietnamese architecture and the country's first university, this temple is a tribute to Confucianism and learning.

- Location: 58 Quoc Tu Giam, Dong Da District (GPS: 21.0285° N, 105.8354° E).
- Opening Hours: 8:00 AM – 5:00 PM.
- Entry Fee: $1–$2.
- Tips: Ideal for photography and quiet reflection.

Afternoon: Lakeside Relaxation

- Hoan Kiem Lake:
  Stroll around this iconic lake and visit the Ngoc Son Temple, located on a small island accessible by the bright red Huc Bridge.
- Entry Fee for Ngoc Son Temple: $1.

West Lake (Ho Tay):

Take a leisurely walk or rent a bike to explore the largest lake in Hanoi. Stop at Tran Quoc Pagoda, a peaceful Buddhist temple along the lake's edge.

Tips: Visit around sunset for breathtaking views.

Estimated Budget

- Transport: $5–$10 (taxis or Grab rides).
- Historical Sites Entry Fees: $2–$3.
- Lunch: $5–$10 at a local restaurant.
- Ngoc Son Temple and Snacks by the Lake: $2–$5.
- Total: $12–$25.

Tips for the Day

- Dress Code: Modest attire for temples and the mausoleum.
- Stay Hydrated: Hanoi can get warm, especially in the afternoons.

- Respect Local Customs: Maintain silence and decorum at religious sites.

Spending the day between Hanoi's historic sites and tranquil lakes is both enriching and restorative, offering insight into the city's culture while allowing time for relaxation.

3. Day 3: A Day Trip to Ha Long Bay or Ninh Binh

Day three offers the perfect opportunity to step out of Hanoi and experience Vietnam's breathtaking natural beauty. Whether you choose the iconic karst landscapes of Ha Long Bay or the lush rice fields and winding waterways of Ninh Binh, both destinations promise unforgettable moments.

Option 1: Ha Long Bay
Ha Long Bay, a UNESCO World Heritage Site, is famed for its emerald waters and towering limestone islands.

- Itinerary Highlights:

Cruise Along the Bay: Join a day cruise to sail among the limestone formations, explore caves, and kayak through serene waters.

- Surprise Cave (Sung Sot Cave): One of the largest and most impressive caves in the bay.
- Titov Island: A short hike offers panoramic views of the bay.

Logistics:
- Distance from Hanoi: 2.5–3.5 hours by bus.
- Tour Operators:
  1. Indochina Junk

     Website: (http://www.indochina-junk.com).

     Contact: +84 24 3933 6260.
  2. Bhaya Cruises

     Website: http://www.bhayacruises.com).

     Contact: +84 24 3944 6777.

Costs:
- Day tour: $50–$90 (includes transport, lunch, and activities).

Option 2: Ninh Binh

Known as the "Inland Ha Long Bay," Ninh Binh boasts a mix of natural beauty and cultural heritage.

Itinerary Highlights:

- Trang An Boat Tour: A peaceful ride through caves and lush valleys.
- Bai Dinh Pagoda: A sprawling Buddhist temple complex with panoramic views.
- Tam Coc: A stunning area of limestone cliffs and rice paddies, best explored by boat.

Logistics:

- Distance from Hanoi: 1.5–2 hours by car.
- Tour Operators:
  1. Ninh Binh Getaway
     Website: http://www.ninhbinhgetaway.com).
     Contact: +84 96 955 5225.
  2. Vietnam Nomad Trails
     Website: http://www.vietnamnomadtrails.com).
     Contact: +84 98 889 1122.

Costs:

Day tour: $40–$70 (includes transport, lunch, and activities).

Estimated Budget

- Transport and Tour: $40–$90 depending on destination and package.
- Meals: Typically included, with additional snacks costing $5–$10.
- Optional Tips: $2–$5 for boat rowers or guides.
- Total: $45–$100.

Tips for the Day

- Dress Comfortably: Lightweight clothing and walking shoes.
- Packing List: Sunscreen, hat, water bottle, and a camera.
- Environmental Awareness: Avoid littering and support sustainable tour operators.

Whether you choose Ha Long Bay's iconic waters or Ninh Binh's tranquil landscapes, this day trip will be a highlight of your Hanoi adventure.

4. Day 4: Shopping, Cafés, and Hidden Spots

Hanoi is a treasure trove of experiences for those who love to explore its vibrant markets, charming cafés, and lesser-known corners. Day four is the perfect time to slow down, shop for souvenirs, sip on authentic Vietnamese coffee, and uncover the city's hidden gems.

Morning: Shopping in Hanoi

Hanoi's markets and boutiques offer everything from traditional handicrafts to contemporary designs.

- Dong Xuan Market: The city's largest indoor market, perfect for fabrics, souvenirs, and local snacks.
- Location: 15B Dong Xuan Street, Hoan Kiem District (GPS: 21.0380° N, 105.8476° E).
- Hours: Daily, 6:00 AM – 6:00 PM.
- Tips: Bargain politely, starting at 50% of the asking price.

- Hang Gai Street: Known as Silk Street, this is the place for high-quality silk products and tailored ao dai.
- What to Buy: Scarves, ties, and custom clothing.

Estimated budget for shopping: $10–$50, depending on purchases.

Afternoon: Cafés to Savor

Hanoi's café culture is an essential part of its charm. Spend your afternoon sampling coffee in unique settings.

- Cafe Giang: Home of the famous egg coffee, a rich and creamy delight.
- Location: 39 Nguyen Huu Huan Street, Hoan Kiem District (GPS: 21.0334° N, 105.8510° E).
- Cost: $1.50–$2.

- The Note Coffee: A colorful café where visitors leave handwritten notes on every surface.
- Location: 64 Luong Van Can Street, Hoan Kiem District (GPS: 21.0312° N, 105.8501° E).
- Cost: $2–$5 for coffee or tea.

Estimated budget for café visits: $5–$10.

Evening: Hidden Spots to Explore

- Train Street: Watch trains pass by while enjoying a drink at a nearby café.
- Tips: Visit around 5:00 PM for train schedules and a lively atmosphere.

- Long Bien Bridge: Take a peaceful evening stroll along this historic steel bridge overlooking the Red River.
- Cost: Free.

Total Estimated Budget
- Shopping: $10–$50.
- Cafés: $5–$10.
- Transport: $5–$10 (Grab rides or taxis).
- Total: $20–$70.

Tips for the Day
- Pack Light: A tote bag for purchases and comfortable walking shoes are essential.
- Stay Safe: Watch your belongings in crowded markets.
- Interact with Locals: Vendors and café owners often share interesting stories about Hanoi's culture.

Day four allows you to immerse yourself in Hanoi's unique charm through its markets, cafés, and hidden corners, creating lasting memories and connections to the city.

5. Day 5: Farewell Hanoi – A Relaxing Morning Before Departure

Your final day in Hanoi is the perfect time to soak in the city's tranquility and reflect on the memories you've made. Start your morning with a leisurely experience, indulge in one last taste of Vietnamese cuisine, and prepare for your journey home.

Morning: A Gentle Start

Hoan Kiem Lake: Begin your day with a peaceful stroll around this iconic lake. The early morning hours offer a serene atmosphere, with locals practicing tai chi or walking briskly along the paths. Stop by the Ngoc Son Temple for a quiet moment of reflection.

- Cost: Free for the stroll; $1 for temple entry.
- Tips: Arrive before 8:00 AM for the calmest experience.

Breakfast at a Café:
- Cafe Dinh: Enjoy a final egg coffee with views of the bustling streets below.
- Location: 13 Dinh Tien Hoang Street, Hoan Kiem District.
- Cost: $1.50–$2.

- Banh Cuon Hang Ga: Savor a light Vietnamese breakfast of steamed rice rolls.
- Location: 14 Hang Ga Street.
- Cost: $2–$3.

Packing and Preparation

After breakfast, return to your hotel to pack and organize your belongings. If you've purchased souvenirs, ensure they're safely packed for transport. Confirm your flight details and allow ample time to check out of your accommodation.

Transport to Noi Bai International Airport

Options:
- Taxi or Grab: Approximately $15–$20 for a 45-minute ride.
- Airport Shuttle Bus: Budget-friendly at $5 per person, departing from central locations like Hanoi Opera House.

Estimated Budget
- Breakfast and Morning Stroll: $3–$5.
- Transport to Airport: $5–$20.
- Total: $10–$25.

Tips for the Day

- Keep Essentials Handy: Passport, tickets, and travel documents should be easily accessible.
- Check Flight Times: Hanoi traffic can be unpredictable, so leave for the airport early.
- Carry Small Bills: Handy for tipping or last-minute purchases.

A Thoughtful Farewell

As you leave Hanoi, reflect on its vibrant energy, rich culture, and warm hospitality. A relaxing final morning is the perfect way to bid farewell to a city that has shared its soul with you, ensuring your journey home is as memorable as your time here.

CHAPTER 10

Insider Tips and Resources

Preparing for a trip to Hanoi? This chapter equips you with essential insights, from packing tips tailored to Hanoi's seasons to apps for navigating the city like a local. Learn how to respect cultural norms and access vital contacts, ensuring your visit is smooth, respectful, and thoroughly enjoyable.

1. Seasonal Packing Guide for Hanoi

Packing for Hanoi means considering its distinct seasons, each offering a different experience. Whether you're visiting in the cool, vibrant spring or the humid summer, this guide ensures you're prepared for all weather conditions. Here's a breakdown of essentials for men, women, kids, and solo travelers.

- Spring (March to May) and Autumn (September to November)
- Weather: Mild and pleasant, with temperatures ranging from 20–25°C (68–77°F).

- For Everyone: Lightweight clothing such as T-shirts, comfortable pants or skirts, and a light jacket for cooler mornings and evenings.
- Shoes: Comfortable walking shoes are a must, as exploring Hanoi often involves cobblestone streets and uneven paths.

Extras:
- Men: Casual shirts and shorts for daytime; a light sweater for evenings.
- Women: Long dresses or breathable trousers; a scarf for added warmth and modesty in temples.
- Kids: Easy-to-layer outfits and a hat for sun protection.

Summer (June to August)
- Weather: Hot and humid, with frequent rain showers. Temperatures can reach 35°C (95°F).
- For Everyone: Pack breathable fabrics like cotton or linen, and opt for light colors to stay cool.
- Shoes: Waterproof footwear or sandals for rainy days.

Extras:
- Men: Quick-dry shorts and a lightweight rain jacket.

- Women: Flowing dresses, comfortable tops, and a compact umbrella.
- Kids: A lightweight raincoat and extra changes of clothing for unexpected rain.

Winter (December to February)

- Weather: Cool to chilly, with temperatures around 10–20°C (50–68°F).
- For Everyone: Layered clothing is key—pack sweaters, long-sleeve shirts, and a warm jacket.
- Shoes: Closed-toe shoes or boots for warmth.

Extras:

- Men: A scarf and gloves for colder nights.
- Women: Thermal leggings and a stylish coat.
- Kids: Thick socks, warm hats, and mittens for added comfort.

General Essentials for Solo Travelers

- A small backpack for daily use.
- Travel-size toiletries.
- Power bank for phones and devices.

Extra Tips

- Modesty matters in Hanoi's temples and historical sites. Carry a shawl or scarf to cover shoulders if needed.

- Always pack sunscreen, sunglasses, and a reusable water bottle regardless of the season.

Being prepared for Hanoi's weather ensures a comfortable trip filled with rich experiences, no matter the season.

2. Apps and Tools for a Seamless Trip

Traveling to Hanoi can be even more enjoyable with the right apps and tools to make your trip smoother and stress-free. From navigating bustling streets to discovering hidden gems, these apps are your trusted companions in Vietnam's capital.

Navigation Apps
- Google Maps: Reliable for walking, driving, and public transport directions. Use it to explore Hanoi's winding streets and find lesser-known spots.
- Maps.me: Great for offline use. Download Hanoi's map in advance and never worry about losing your way.

Language and Communication
- Google Translate: An essential tool for bridging language barriers. Use the voice or text feature to communicate with locals or translate signs and menus.

- Duolingo: Learn basic Vietnamese phrases before your trip to make interactions more meaningful.

Transport Apps

- Grab: The go-to ride-hailing app for taxis, motorbikes, and even food delivery. It's affordable, convenient, and widely used in Hanoi.
- BusMap: If you're planning to use Hanoi's public buses, this app provides accurate routes, schedules, and fare information.

Accommodation and Planning

- Booking.com: Ideal for finding accommodations ranging from budget-friendly hostels to luxurious hotels.
- Airbnb: Perfect for unique stays like homestays or serviced apartments in Hanoi's vibrant neighborhoods.

Food and Dining

- Foody: A local app that acts as a guide to Hanoi's food scene. Find highly rated street food stalls, restaurants, and cafés with user reviews.
- HappyCow: Excellent for vegetarian or vegan travelers looking for plant-based options in the city.

Currency and Budgeting

- XE Currency: Keep track of currency exchange rates and convert Vietnamese Dong to your home currency easily.

- Splitwise: Handy for group travelers to manage shared expenses, ensuring everyone pays their fair share.

Cultural Insights
- Vietnam Travel Guide by Triposo: Offline travel information including cultural tips, itineraries, and must-see landmarks.
- YouTube: Follow travel vloggers for local recommendations and insights about Hanoi before or during your trip.

Extras
- VPN App: Stay secure while using public Wi-Fi in cafés or hotels.
- Zalo: A popular local messaging app that can help you connect with tour guides or local businesses.

Equipping yourself with these apps ensures your time in Hanoi is smooth, enjoyable, and enriched with memorable experiences.

3. How to Respect Local Customs and Culture

Hanoi is a city rich in history and tradition, where respecting local customs enhances your travel experience and shows appreciation for the community. Understanding a few cultural norms can make your interactions more meaningful and leave a positive impression.

1. Dress Modestly
When visiting temples, pagodas, or other sacred sites, ensure your attire is respectful. Avoid shorts, tank tops, or revealing clothing. For women, carrying a light scarf to cover shoulders is a good idea. Comfortable yet modest outfits are also appreciated in rural areas or during formal events.

2. Greetings and Communication
A polite nod or a slight bow is a customary way to greet someone, especially elders or in formal settings. Handshakes are becoming common, but always use both hands or support your handshake with your left hand for added respect. Learn simple phrases like "Xin chào" (hello) and "Cảm ơn" (thank you) to connect better with locals.

3. Temple Etiquette

When entering a temple or pagoda, remove your shoes before stepping inside. Keep your voice low, and avoid pointing directly at statues or people. Always walk behind seated worshippers and refrain from taking photos unless permission is clearly indicated.

4. Respect Meal Customs

If you're invited to a local's home, bring a small gift like fruits or sweets as a gesture of gratitude. Wait for the host to invite you to eat before starting, and use both hands when passing dishes. Leaving a small amount of food on your plate is polite, signifying you're satisfied.

5. Street Etiquette

Hanoi's bustling streets may seem overwhelming, but crossing roads with confidence and awareness is key. When taking photos, ask permission if locals are part of your shot, particularly street vendors or performers.

6. Avoid Sensitive Topics

Conversations about politics or sensitive historical events should be approached carefully or avoided altogether. It's best to listen and learn rather than offering strong opinions.

7. Support Local Businesses

Shop at local markets, eat at family-owned restaurants, and support artisans to give back to the community while enjoying an authentic experience.

8. Be Patient

Hanoi's pace can be energetic, and things may not always go as planned. A friendly attitude and patience go a long way in forming genuine connections.

Respecting Hanoi's customs shows your thoughtfulness and helps you experience the city with warmth and authenticity. It's a simple way to create positive memories for yourself and those you meet along the way.

4. Contact Directory: Embassies, Hospitals, and Tourist Assistance

Having essential contacts at your fingertips ensures peace of mind while traveling. Whether you need help with a lost passport, medical assistance, or guidance, Hanoi provides reliable resources for visitors. Here's a quick guide to the key contacts you may need.

Embassies in Hanoi

If you lose important travel documents or require consular services, your embassy can provide assistance. Some major embassies in Hanoi include:

United States Embassy

Address: 7 Lang Ha Street, Ba Dinh District

Phone: +84 24 3850 5000

Website: http://vn.usembassy.gov)

United Kingdom Embassy

Address: Central Building, 31 Hai Ba Trung Street, Hoan Kiem District

Phone: +84 24 3936 0500

Website: http://www.gov.uk/world/vietnam)

Australia Embassy

Address: 8 Dao Tan Street, Ba Dinh District

Phone: +84 24 3774 0100

Website: http://vietnam.embassy.gov.au)

Check your own country's embassy for updated contact details.

Hospitals and Medical Assistance

For medical emergencies or routine care, Hanoi has reputable hospitals catering to international visitors.

Hanoi Family Medical Practice

Address: 298 I Kim Ma Street, Ba Dinh District

Phone: +84 24 3843 0748

Services: 24/7 emergency care, English-speaking staff, general practice, and specialist consultations.

Vinmec International Hospital

Address: 458 Minh Khai Street, Hai Ba Trung District

Phone: +84 24 3974 3556

Services: Modern facilities with a focus on patient care and advanced treatments.

Tourist Assistance

For lost belongings, navigating the city, or other queries, Hanoi provides several support options.

Tourist Police (Hoan Kiem District)

Phone: +84 24 3939 6250

Services: Assistance for tourists in distress or resolving minor issues.

Tourist Information Center

Address: 28 Hang Dau Street, Hoan Kiem District

Phone: +84 24 3926 3366

Services: Maps, travel advice, and tips for exploring Hanoi.

Helpful Tips

- Keep Copies: Store copies of your passport and important documents in case of loss.
- Save Numbers: Program these contacts into your phone for quick access.
- Know Your Insurance: Confirm your travel insurance covers medical costs in Vietnam.

Hanoi's resources are here to ensure you feel safe and supported throughout your trip, letting you enjoy your journey with confidence.

CONCLUSION

Hanoi isn't just a city you visit; it's a place you feel deeply. Its vibrant streets, steeped in history and alive with energy, offer a unique rhythm that blends tradition with modernity. From the aroma of freshly brewed coffee in quaint cafés to the hum of motorbikes weaving through ancient streets, Hanoi leaves an imprint on your senses.

Walking through the Old Quarter feels like stepping into a living museum, where each turn reveals hidden treasures. Historical landmarks like the Ho Chi Minh Mausoleum and Temple of Literature connect you to Vietnam's rich past, while tranquil spots like Hoan Kiem Lake and West Lake provide the perfect balance for moments of reflection.

The flavors of Hanoi are unforgettable. Whether you're savoring a steaming bowl of pho at a street-side stall, biting into a perfectly crafted banh mi, or indulging in a creamy egg coffee, the city's cuisine is a journey in itself. Each dish tells a story, blending age-old recipes with the warmth of local hospitality.

Beyond the landmarks and food, what truly defines Hanoi is its people. Their warmth, resilience, and pride in their heritage shine through in every interaction. Whether it's a vendor helping you navigate a bustling market, a guide sharing local legends, or a friendly café owner teaching you a few Vietnamese phrases, these moments of connection are what make Hanoi unforgettable.

As you leave Hanoi, you'll carry more than souvenirs—you'll take with you memories of sunsets over Long Bien Bridge, the melody of temple bells, and the quiet beauty of lantern-lit streets at night. Hanoi invites you not only to see its sights but to feel its soul, making it a city that doesn't just impress but leaves a lasting imprint.

So, whether you've just started planning or are looking forward to a return trip, know that Hanoi will welcome you with open arms and an open heart. It's not just a place to explore—it's a place to connect, reflect, and fall in love with life in its simplest and most beautiful form.

Printed in Great Britain
by Amazon

034f46c4-6641-47c5-b308-8a424b7a12c5R01